Gold Mining in the Pit of Sorrow

A Journey Through Child Loss and Grief

By William W. Gaskill

xulon
PRESS

www.xulonpress.com

For Jonathan Mayne Gaskill

April 10th, 1981-July 23rd, 2005

"May you build a ladder up to the stars,
May you climb on every rung,
And may you stay forever young"

Bob Dylan

Gold Mining in the Pit of Sorrow

Introduction

What follows is one man's chronicle of the heart cries and struggles, the prayers, and as my wife Jean has been dutiful to remind me, the distorted memories of the journey of grief through the loss of a child, in this instance, the life of my youngest son Jon. I say distorted, because she remembers the events that occurred differently, in factual detail and in emotional timbre. To compound the difficulties even further, this is an account of my own grieving plus my interpretation of my wife's as I have lived so closely with her. My perceptions of where she has been and what she has been feeling may or may not be accurate; they are simply how it all felt to me at the time. Were you to ask Jean if what I am reporting is accurate, she would surely say something like, "No that's not how it was at all."

Part of the difference between us surely lies in the fact that I am grieving as a man and a father. She is experiencing her grief as a mother. It was Jean who carried Jon in her womb, delivered him into the world, and nursed him at her breast. No man alive knows much about such things beyond our powers to imagine what it might be like, and these are very limited powers indeed.

One of my favorite writers is Danish theologian Soren Kierkegaard who said that theological truth should be held as lightly as one would hold the head of a thistle. This is how I have tried to hold my awareness of Jean's sorrow, delicately, patiently, and respectfully. I have tried not to impose my expectations for her comfort or recovery upon her. I have sought to be a source of support and comfort to her as far as possible and to trust the Spirit to bring her through to the place she needs to be.

Undaunted by these problems of disparity in our recollection, I have apologized to Jean, told her to write her own book, and have stubbornly pressed on with my account. It really matters little to me if I got a fact or two wrong or if I have placed it in incorrect order from how it actually happened. With what I've been through it's a wonder that my memory is working at all. I find it a matter for singular unconcern if my scrambled brain has rearranged a few things. The story unfolds here as I remember it and to the best of my ability I have tried to be accurate, but more importantly, to be honest.

Child loss plunges one into a prolonged condition of living emotionally and spiritually overloaded. Grief functions like a prism that can bend things in odd directions in many unpredictable ways. What I discovered early was that I was nowhere near being in charge. This would not be something I could control, direct, or manage in any way. This grief had, and still has, a life of its own. It comes and goes at will from a place beyond my will. It comes in times, places, and at an intensity that can neither be predicted nor planned. When it comes, I've learned to acknowledge its presence, give it its due, and pay attention to see what I can learn. I call this gold mining in the pit of sorrow.

Mining for gold is much different than panning for gold. Some of the early prospectors discovered that they could find gold merely by scooping up gravel from a running stream and sorting through what they had in their pan. The risks were few and the work could be done in the full light of day. It is not so with mining. Gold mining means digging a pit and going down, down, down, into a shaft both dark and dangerous. The risks are severe and the casualties numerous. Gold mining takes courage and determination. To find gold in the pit of sorrow caused by the loss of a child does not come cheaply nor can the search be done without a conscious determination to go after precious metal.

I am a follower of Christ. Since coming to him in my early twenties, I have been committed to the truth that life is stronger than death. Jesus' resurrection from the grave establishes that for me. It is the central linchpin of Christian faith. So, fairly soon after Jon died, in that intense season where death strutted across the stage of my life and the lives of all who loved and cared for Jon, crowing that a great victory had been won, I knew that the gauntlet had been thrown down in front of my faith. I would now get the chance to discover if what I believed could stand the intense heat that waited in this furnace of affliction.

There is gold in this pit, but the only way to find it is to press into the sorrow. The only way its true value can be possessed is if it is purified by fire. Being thrust into this furnace has taught me both courage and humility gained at levels impossible to fathom at lesser grades of intensity. The depth of the sorrow has yielded a more pure grade of gold. It became intolerable to me to cede any uncontested ground to the despair that grief was peddling. No sale! I determined to press past the pretense that death is the ultimate reality and find the truth embedded in the seams of precious metal between the layers of sorrow's shale and granite. If my faith could not stand the heat there, deep in the ground, and if the gold could not submit to the refiner's fire, then what good was it really? And if I failed to find gold, death's taunts would go unanswered and Jon would have been just another victim who died to no purpose.

I write what follows as a believer still. I hope you share my faith, but possibly you don't. My purpose here is not to convert anyone since only God can do that. This is not an attempt to write a theology of suffering or to explain the great mysteries of our difficult life here. As I said above it is simply a journal of one man's wrestling match with an overwhelming loss. It is not intended to be a book of answers so much as an account of one who sought enough courage to summon into the light of day some of the questions that haunted his own soul. Should you insist that it be anything more, you will be irritated at best.

My prayer is that, whether or not you believe the Bible story of God's love and saving work done for us through Jesus Christ, what I share in the following pages may serve to lighten your load in some small way if you are hurting as I myself have been.

In the early months after Jon died I read many books on death, dying, and grief, a number of which were not written by people of faith, though many were. Each one yielded some helpful insight or two that carried me along a step or two further. Each insight was like a tiny treasure that I would tuck away and I would keep on going. Hopefully you will find a gold nugget or two here.

The season of reading eventually came to an end. I found after a while that the returns were diminishing, and I got tired of being told to share my feelings, which I readily did with anyone who would listen. One soon discovers that real and patient listeners, listeners who are with you for the long haul, are few and the well of volunteers for that duty soon runs dry. I can remember coming to the point of irritation; "Okay, I've shared my feelings and I still feel like hell. What else do you have for me?" And I thought, "How long can I keep subjecting my friends who are willing to listen to what soon became a repetitive rehearsal of the conditions of my sadness?"

As a pastor, I made a conscious decision not to make every sermon about my grief. The congregation deserved more than a steady diet of my soul's travails and I tried to be disciplined in this regard, though the grief leaked out and seasoned everything I said and did, whether it was preaching, teaching, counseling, or other types of pastoral care. There were many days during the first year, days that I called "sad days" when I went to my study intending to work but found myself paralyzed by my sorrow and unable to do much. Fortunately for me, my job has great flexibility, so I could simply leave and do something else. I found myself wondering how in the world others in my situation but lacking my flexibility survived this.

And speaking of them, I soon discovered how many of us there are. I soon realized that there had been many all around me, even some of my own parishioners, who had lost children, some more than one. They passed by, unobtrusively buried in their own private hells, mute as well as courageous, carrying their broken hearts with dignity and resolve to go on living, even if they did not feel like it. Over time, I became aware of the conventional wisdom that says children should bury their parents but parents should never have to bury their children, as though the old have some sort of entitlement against this particular sorrow. This surely is a peculiar notion of our age.

This really struck home for me when I was visiting my oldest son Mark at his home in western Pennsylvania. Like me, Mark is a Presbyterian pastor, he in a small town closely surrounded by farmland and open country. On the hill just above his home, surrounded by woods and fields, is a small country cemetery. One day I decided to walk around in it and read the inscriptions on the gravestones. In more than one spot, there are rows of little graves, children of families who probably got the flu or some such disease before the age of antibiotics and modern medicine. It dawned on me that in times past, child loss was neither an unusual nor even an unexpected event. It was a fact of life. People surely had no sense that it was an experience which they were entitled to avoid as we in our day seem to believe. I'm guessing that the sorrow was no less devastating nevertheless.

I think it is fair for you to know the suppositional basis for my point of view, so I have stated openly here that I am a believer in the Gospel of Jesus Christ. If you are reading because you have now joined the club that no parent wants to join, my guess is that your faith, if you have it, has come under an unprecedented assault. The only thing I can say is that I have experienced the helping hand of God in many ways large and small. I am like a voice crying in the wilderness, "Prepare ye the way of the Lord. Make his paths straight."

I still believe and I'm still standing, though I do now walk with a limp as most do who dare to wrestle with The Angel of the Lord until daybreak as did the Hebrew patriarch Jacob so long ago. The angel touched the strongest bone in Jacob's body and put it out of joint. You can read the story in the 32nd chapter of Genesis.

The grief of child loss will touch you, even where you think yourself most impregnable and will cause you to become well acquainted with any hidden weakness you heretofore had tucked away out of sight from yourself and others.

The effects of grief are not simply emotional and spiritual either. Grief made its presence known viscerally in me as well. Beginning in the Fall after Jon's death in July, I began to have pronounced weakness in my thighs. It became hard to go up and down stairs of any kind, or to climb a ladder or just to play with my grandchildren. I had no bounce in my step, and even walking was a chore. It wasn't exactly painful; I just had very little strength.

I developed chest pains and spent hours wondering if this were a heart attack, but heart attack veterans described the pain as unbearably intense, leaving no doubt. My pain was regular but more annoying than intense. Perhaps grief had affected my breathing. I heard that stress could make a person gulp air instead of breathing smoothly and cause heartburn-like symptoms in the chest. And I would have bouts of heart arrhythmia from time to time, especially when I lay down to go to sleep.

These were all things going bump in the night Early on, they provided enough wakefulness which I would use to run the film in my mind of the events of the night Jon died, which I did over and over until I decided to stop. I told no one of any of this because I am the ultimate medical coward, white coat syndrome is the more dignified title for my cowardice, a condition over which I seemed to have no control. I didn't want the added pressure from people who loved me who I was sure would badger me to go to the doctor. It was better just to suffer in silence and keep my fears to myself.

I developed high blood pressure and began to take medicine daily. I wondered out loud to my doctor (yes, I did finally go), if this could be a result of grief. He said it may have been possible.

I tried to buy some life insurance. There was a slight abnormality in the home administered EKG. I went to the doctor who sent me for a stress test which could not be completed because I had a panic attack mid-way through it. I was referred to a cardiologist who said as far as he could see, concern was unwarranted. Whether any of this was directly caused by grief is anybody's guess. But I can't rule it out. Obviously, I've survived it.

Maybe you are struggling toward the dawn, clinging like Jacob to whatever messenger God has sent your way and refusing to let go until a blessing is bestowed. I invite you to walk along with me for a little stretch of the road of sorrow. Maybe you will find something of value. Maybe like Jacob who became Israel at the end of the long night, you too will get a name change, a down payment for a change in your character. Jacob's name was changed from "Grabber" to "Grappler with God." The name was changed after a night. The change in character took more time. But the change did come. Maybe a gold nugget will catch your eye as it reflects the light of the Son. In any event, I wish you deep consolation from the God of all comfort.

Chapter I

Big Joe

"No one has greater love than this, to lay down one's life for one's friends."

John 15:13

I became a Christian because of the death of someone else's son. Joe and I met during our second year in "Happy Valley" on the campus of Penn State University. Big Joe was nick named because he was big, and there was another Joe in the crowd who was physically smaller whom we called "Little Joe." Joe had a wide smile and a big heart as well. There were about twenty of us who formed a small band of late sixties hippies. Most of us drank deeply from the wells of the waters of the overall sense of alienation of the period and carried the wounds of our misguided attempts to resolve the pain of our malaise for many years to come.

A year after we met, Joe was diagnosed as having MS. He began to be a little unsteady on his feet and to experience blurred vision. Soon he was wearing a patch over one eye, a modern day pirate. We dabbled in the study of Buddhism and meditation, ate natural foods, baked bread, and tried to cover the inner emptiness in any way we could. Once in a while, we even went to class. I would say, "Hey, Big Joe, how ya doing," and he'd reply, "Aw, you know man, just passing time in the void." We didn't yet know that the time was so short and the void was neither passive nor benign.

We liked to go camping in the forest south of State College at a site in a little saddle of land just a stone's throw from the edge of a cliff that looked out over an idyllic Pennsylvania valley with Spruce Creek riffling down below. It was truly a majestic scene and we used to fantasize that when the world was coming to an end we would all meet here and leave together.

During my final term, I had a theater arts project to make a film. I checked out the 16 mm. film camera and we headed off to the cliff. When we arrived, I was below my friends, four or five of them as I remember, including Joe poised on the face of the mountain, with me perched below in position to film. The camera was rolling.

Suddenly, Joe stumbled. I asked if he were okay and he said he was fine. I said that I didn't want to lose him for a stupid film project. He assured me he was okay. In hindsight, perhaps we had received a warning that both of us chose to ignore. Minutes after this final assurance, Big Joe stumbled again and sailed past me disappearing from sight below. My futile attempt to grab him as we went by was a failure. Joe was gone into silent, void space. Our frantic cries calling out his name were met by a dead silence. The void was palpably filled with dread.

We found him on a ledge, maybe a hundred feet below. His life was gone. His skull was fractured. Moisture dripped from cracks in the rocks. Blood dripped from the hole in Big Joe's skull. It was agreed that I would remain with him while the others went for help. My body sat glued to the tiny ledge, Joe's resting place. Time stood still. Flies buzzed in an otherwise deafening quiet. Invisible fingers pressed me to continue Joe's flight in my own body. I resisted. I tried to pray.

Then out of the void came the Voice, not audible but wholly other. In response to my prayers came the stern rebuke which went like this: "You're lying." I tried again, to be more sincere, or perhaps to sound more pathetic. Again, "You're lying. The reason you are lying is that you are incapable of telling the truth. The reason for this is that the truth is not in you. You have a deceitful heart. If you refuse to turn to me, you have no life in you. You are dead already. You can either turn to me for life, you can go through the motions like a dead man walking, or you can go ahead as you are being tempted and finish it all right here by taking the leap. You choose."

I felt the sting of the truth. And I knew I was not just talking to myself, because I would not have talked to myself in that way. For once, my cowardice did me in good stead. I would not leap to my own demise; I would try to hold on.

Bear in mind that I was not a Christian. I knew almost no Bible except what I'd heard in public school in the morning Bible readings, and certainly knew no Christian theology. I was baptized and raised in the Methodist church for as long as my mother could induce me to attend. I was confirmed, after memorizing the Apostle's creed and sitting through some classes absorbing information that I felt was totally irrelevant to my life. Like most adolescents, I found it difficult to concentrate on the significance of the proper use of liturgical colors while in the middle of a hormone storm. I began to look for a way out and would find it soon enough.

The voice was sharp and clear, but as I said, not audible. I was being addressed by one beyond myself and I knew it. I came under a strong conviction of sin, though I wouldn't have known to call it that at the time. Brazenly, I plea bargained with God. "Okay," I said, "I want to give my life to you, if you're truly out there. Please just be sure to make it real. I've followed too much deception already. I've lost my dear friend because of it. I don't want to submit to another falsehood just to conform to conventional religion. Give me something real, *please!*"

Chapter II

Life After a Funeral

J oe's funeral was at his home in McKeesport, a steel mill town adjacent to Pittsburgh. Joe referred to his dad affectionately as a "mill hunk". He was a hard working, blue collar steel worker who wanted a good education for his son and a brighter future than his own. He was like so many fathers of his generation, a bread- winning, no nonsense kind of man. Joe used to humorously boast that the sunsets in McKeesport were a most beautiful red due to the pollution spewing from the mill stacks. Joe's family was Roman Catholic, so I guess the funeral was conducted by a priest. I seem to remember that it was conducted in a funeral parlor, but have no real memory of who was there or what was said. I remember so little about his funeral service because I was numb with both guilt and grief.

Somehow it was arranged that when the family came to collect Joe's things in State College they would go to the cliff to see where their son had fallen to his death. I was to be one of the main guides on this excursion. It was a brutally painful outing. They questioned over and over, "How did it happen," and "Was he on drugs," and what were we doing out here anyway?" They wanted to know in excruciating detail anything we could remember. We had little to offer them at that point. Joe's dad pranced around the edge of the cliff, peering over the edge, trying to see where he had landed, and scaring me to the point of nausea with the specter of a repeat episode.

I'm ashamed to say that from my perspective the experience was mostly about me at that point. I had little awareness really of their agony and their loss. I simply endured the day and was deeply relieved when they pulled away. I felt sorry for them but there was nothing I could do. I had my own grief to live through and the biting memory of the Voice.

Emotionally in the months to come, I suffered grief's depression. Spiritually, I was like a plane circling an airport awaiting directions and permission to land. "God, if you're out there, take my life. I can't handle it anymore." So I had prayed. Would God answer? Was God real? What would such a life given to God look like anyway? I really didn't know the answers.

As my old life lay in tatters and important relationships lay in ruins, I set off with several friends and my future wife to buy land in Arkansas and establish a commune. It was a great adventure to load up in a van and set out into uncharted waters. I eagerly left "unhappy valley" behind. A few days later we crossed the Mississippi River just as a fire-red sun was setting over the steaming, east Arkansas flatlands. It felt like we'd been transported to another country altogether.

By July of the year 1971, we had purchased sixty acres and began work on construction of our geodesic dome. We became a north central Arkansas phenomenon. People came from miles around to see the hippies and their round house. Many of the locals viewed us with suspicion, some with hostility, but then there were the Christians who befriended us. They loved us, accepted us, helped us, gave us advice and loaned us tools. Several even fed us from their own modest means and from their gardens. Their open hearts began to soften my own broken heart, which it turns out was more than ready to receive the grace of Christ.

I had a great prayer person in my family, my father's cousin Margy Graham, who interceded for me faithfully and sent me a newly published Jerusalem Bible. I started reading (by chance?), the book of Ecclesiastes. "How did that get in there?", I asked myself. "All is vanity" said the preacher. Who is this preacher anyway? "And a striving after wind." Why wasn't I told about this? I thought maybe there was more here than met the eye. It was my first inkling that the Bible was more than a rule book written by adults to make sure their children would not have any pleasure or fun in life.

I wrote to my mother who had prayed long and hard. Finally at one point along the way she had decided I wasn't worth speaking to in my state of sin and rebellion. I told her I had begun to read the Bible. She received my letter the very day after she had lain in her bed and cried out to the Lord, "I give up, Lord. He's yours. I can't make him be the man you would have him to be. I surrender him to you." My letter came to her like a lightning strike.

She fired off a response advising me to begin by reading the Gospel of John. I took her advice. By the time I finished reading John, I had a personal relationship with Jesus. I knew him as a living person. In all the years of reflection since, my only explanation for this still is that it is by sheer grace on His part that I have been allowed to know Him as my living Savior and as my friend. A mystical transaction had been accomplished for my benefit. A deep union between his heart and mine had been forged. I had no way of knowing at the time how desperately I would need this unique and tender knowledge of my living Lord. Many years later I would come to know the agony of child loss and I would crave once again to hear the Voice, not in conviction but in consolation.

I became a Christian through the death of someone's son. Big Joe's death drew me to a screeching halt and caused me to change directions. The theologians call this repentance. It was the death of Jesus of Nazareth that brought me to life. I guess you could say it took two lives to turn me spiritually toward home. Joe's was offered in a horrible accident. Jesus' death was no accident.

We say Jesus was slain before the foundation of the world. What we mean is that his death was no afterthought but was completely forethought. The notion of all those centuries of anticipation and actual planning for the event of the cross, Father and Son and Spirit in collusion together, preparing for the rescue of us wayward children, boggles the mind.

How agonizing for the Father to hear the Gethsemane prayer of His own Son, "If it be possible, let this cup pass from me. Nevertheless, not what I will but what you will." How unfathomable to think that His answer had to be, "No Son, it's not possible. You must drink the cup down to the bitter dregs. You will be in so much pain that you will cry in dereliction, a cry so deeply felt that it will pierce my own being as well. You and I will suffer together to bring your brothers and sisters home at last. It is the appointed way and we must walk it together."

My heavenly Father knows more about child loss than I ever will. Not only has he endured the crucifixion of His one and only begotten Son, he has witnessed the sin tormented existence of countless of his created children. Most of us fathers and mothers would, if given the choice, sacrifice our own lives if it meant the saving of our child. We would do it for love. Those of us who have endured the loss of a child would do it as well to avoid living through this all encompassing grief that is akin to being swallowed alive by a monster from the deep.

God did do it for salvation. God did do it for love. God has provided for us a way to get home from here, home to our Father's house. God did not hold back what was most precious to God, the life of God's own son. How shall we assign value to this, except to accept the gift with great gratitude. We have no suitable resources to offer in payment, so in humility and wonder, we offer our hearts. Sadly though, God's heart is repeatedly pierced as so many offer him only a stiff neck and a hard heart and a back turned as they wander off in the opposite direction, away from home and into the wilderness of sin.

Not long ago, I thought of Big Joe's mom and dad for the first time in many years, probably for the first time with any understanding. My guess is that they are long gone from this world and have already been reunited with their son. If they were still here and I was given the opportunity to write them a letter, it would go something like this:

Dear Mr. and Mrs. H,

I'm sure you don't remember me, but I counted your son Joseph, "Big Joe", as one of my dearest friends. His death was a tragic loss to me and I had no ability at the time to see beyond my own pain and to empathize with yours. For this stupidity, I ask your forgiveness.

I can only hope and believe that the Lord found others who could come along side you both with some measure of comfort, though I know now that the core of this experience of losing a child is deeply isolating. I now know this first hand since I have grown, have become a father of three children of my own, and lost the youngest of my sons to the scourge of drug addiction. There are places in our grief that none other can access and we endure these terrible regions of the heart alone.

I have continued to hold Joe in my heart these many years as I know you have too. I want you to know that God used Joe's death to turn my life around and to save me from a life of profligacy and self destruction. I know this in no way makes up for your loss.

It is because of Joe that I have a deeply personal under-standing of how the death of one issues in life for another. Joe's death has shown me the pattern of life, death, and resurrection that is at the heart of my faith in Jesus Christ. Joe's death was an accident which Christ transformed into an offering where I was concerned. He was precious to me both in life and in death.

I want to thank you for presenting him, loved and nurtured, into the world. I pray that you have now been reunited with Joe, that you have found one another in that place where every tear is wiped away and where death is no more, nor mourning, nor crying, because the former things have passed away.

Sincerely yours,
Bill G.

Chapter III

Disaster

Prayers for the beginning:

God, help me!

Lord, have mercy!

Jesus! I hurt too badly to pray. Hear my anguished cries!

Why God? Why?

We heard Jon come in around 2 AM. Jean had become accustomed to sleeping lightly until he had gotten home, if she slept at all. The door would rattle. We'd hear some noise in the kitchen below our bedroom, and then hear Jon bound down to his basement bedroom. On almost every night, I would be awakened by the quiet sound of Jean getting up and going downstairs to talk and spend some time with Jon in the middle of the night. On this night, she was simply too tired to arise.

At 3 AM, the backyard foliage was still reflecting the light from Jon's room. Neither of us was sleeping. Jean got up to investigate. Moments later, her voice rose two flights of stairs to meet my ears. There was a quality of distress and panic that I had never heard in Jean's voice in all our years together. "Jon's in trouble! I think he's O D'd!" I quickly pulled on my jeans and went downstairs. Jean was frantic. John was still in a sitting position on the edge of his mattress. When Jean found him, he was still holding a bottle of water in one hand and had a syringe tucked in the fingers of his other hand like a cigarette.

I told Jean to call 911 which she did. I laid Jon down on the rug. There was a mixture of saliva and blood around his mouth. I felt his carotid artery. There was no pulse. I yelled his name a few times. He was gone. I said to Jean, "I think he's gone." The statement didn't really register. The atmosphere was surreal. She was already in shock and in horror. Our worst fear had finally come upon us. Our beautiful baby boy was dead.

Chapter IV

Before the Fall

"The easiest thing of all is to die; the difficult thing is to live."

Soren Kierkegaard

Jon is the youngest of our three. I was there when he was born. He was late arriving but came in a hurry. I was barely able to get togged in hospital gown and paper shoe covers and make it into the delivery room in time. I saw them swab him off at birth and lay him upon Jean's breast. He was an adorable delight to us both.

Jon was full of energy and seemed to live life in a hurry from the day of his birth. He never walked through the house. He ran everywhere. Perhaps he was born to run. My mother called him a mosquito, always buzzing around, at times stirring a strong temptation to swat by surrounding adults. They never did however. We mostly just rolled our eyes and marveled.

Jon was a born extrovert, handsome and charismatic. Females of all ages instantly adored him. He broke hearts along the way of his brief life. I often referred to him as a "chick magnet" because he was truly magnetic to members of the opposite sex. He had a heart for adventure along with the cockiness of youth. He mistakenly believed he could handle anything and tried most everything that came his way. His greatest strength was also his fatal flaw. The belief among youth that they are indestructible is a serious miscalculation made by many. It often leads to serious trouble, and in Jon's case, it led to his death.

Early in life, Jon was a natural athlete. He loved anything that was a sport and he relished competition. He played basketball, baseball, and ran cross country. He mastered the skateboard, the skim-board, and finally his great love became surfing. He took a trip to Tonga, all by himself at 21 years of age, to try surfing in the big waves. With not a little apprehension and for my part a great deal of admiration, we dropped him off at Newark International Airport for his excursion that would take him half way around the world and back.

While in Tonga, he got sunburned as never before, got dashed against coral reefs leaving large scrape marks on his torso, and was finally forced to admit that perhaps the waves in the south Pacific were a bit larger than he could handle given his skill level as a surfer. He got in a fight with some Aussies in Tonga who were bullying another surfer. That stirred the fires of Jon's soul who loved to champion the underdog so he took care of it with his fists, though by nature he was not violent.

I remember picking him up around midnight at the Newark airport when he returned. He was ripe indeed. The combination of surf, sand, sweat, and salt, plus the lack of adequate shower facilities on the far off island had transformed my son into an aromatic stinker. It must have been a very long flight for those around him in the planes coming home.

Driving south on the New Jersey turnpike in the wee hours, I kept opening the vent and cracking the window to get some fresh air, which caused the windshield to fog up. To resist utter asphyxiation I was forced to alternate between defroster and vent all the way down the highway until we reached home. It was a Catch 22 situation between driving blind or dying of an over-ripe surfer's odor. I was so proud of his courage and his spirit of adventure and so glad when he took a shower. My young son was developing into a real man!

Though clever and bright, Jon had some learning disabilities, or should I say he just didn't learn in the conventional ways, so the public schools did not really know how to educate him. Their response to this condition was to recommend giving Jon drugs. We steadfastly resisted the attempts to put Jon on Ritalin for many years. He did try it for a short spell when he was in high school but didn't like its effects and soon discontinued its use.

Jon had a heart of compassion and a strong sense of loyalty. What he lacked was wisdom in how to apply these gifts in a way that would not be self-destructive. He expressed loyalty to his rebellious sister by getting involved in some of her worst habits. Jon ran with a fast crowd and became facile at developing and maintaining a double life; there was the one he showed us and the one he actually lived. I instinctively knew what he was up to because that's exactly what I had done at his age. I'd made a vow to myself as a dad that I would never let my kids do to me what I had done to my parents, but in the end I didn't know how to prevent it. Each of us has this terrifying freedom which is a great blessing when redeemed but which issues in great destructiveness when we are still fallen.

Chapter V

Into the Web

Jon made it through to high school graduation, and then opted to become a plumber. He completed the five years of class work and was an apprentice within a loosely run company which employed a number of people abusing alcohol and drugs. He instantly was making big money and doing well in his new trade. He was also slipping into bondage.

Jon moved in with a young woman and her mother, who fostered their cohabitation. He and his new mate became drug buddies together in a codependent dance of addiction. Both she and her mother systematically manipulated him by playing on his innate loyalty to get things they wanted. They undermined his self esteem by constantly assaulting him with his inadequacies.

I still don't know when Jon moved from recreational drug taking to hard addicting drugs. I think he was prescribed oxycotin as a painkiller following his first of two collapsed lungs. After recovery, he just kept on going, developing a $700 per week habit, which he supported with plumbing money, easy credit, and sponging off us on a regular basis. Jon could play his mom's heart strings like a fiddle and did so repeatedly to get what he wanted.

He bought a brand new pickup truck which I had advised against. Then he bought a new work van because he didn't want to drive the company's van. I had forbidden him to buy a motorcycle while living at home with me. He came home with one anyway. I was being dishonored in my own home; at least that was how I felt. I was mostly furious at what I could see but could not change. Jon had successfully engaged Jean to be the emotional buffer between us, building an emotional triangle which I felt powerless to deconstruct. This served to deepen my chronic sense of aggravation.

Finally, when the money got tight, Jon resorted to heroin as a cheaper alternative. His life spiraled downward and we lacked the ability to stop his free fall. Creditors began to call relentlessly on our number. We received at least ten calls a day. Threatening letters would arrive almost daily in the mail. The car dealer called to warn that the repo man was poised to snatch Jon's pickup truck for lack of making timely payments. His debt on our credit cards was steadily mounting. Always sincere and pleading, Jean had trouble resisting the plaintive cries of her little boy.

Anyone who has lived with a beloved addict knows it is a living hell. With ever increasing frequency, addicts break their promises to themselves and to the people who love them most. They become chronic and habitual liars as the addiction breeds an ever intensifying need to live deceitfully. They become more and more manipulative and cagey. Their addiction becomes the driving force in their existence and they indulge in all kinds of "stinking thinking" to justify what they do to themselves and others. Those who love them have a hard time believing just how bad this all is, nor can they imagine how things have fallen so far so fast.

I knew my son and I knew my son on drugs. They were not the same people at all. He did not eat properly. His bodily functions were all out of whack. The hours he kept were chaotic. When he lived at home he could not be roused to go to work. The owners of his company fostered and enabled this all by permitting it to continue. The web of enabling and co-dependency was far flung enough to allow Jon to continue on toward self destruction.

It was on my birthday, May 17th, 2004 that Jon admitted that he was in trouble. What had been planned as a celebration became a watershed into a nightmare. Together we hopped on a fourteen month roller coaster ride that saw us all oscillate between addiction and recovery and relapse in a repeated pattern. We swung wildly between hope and despair. Up and down we went like prisoners trapped inside some demonic yo yo. People prayed. We prayed. I raged. I forgave. I spent time. I spent money. On four or five occasions Jon had an opiate blocking pellet surgically implanted in his arm in an attempt to get clean. They cost $700 apiece, which we gladly paid. They provided a six week window each time for Jon to break the cycle of addiction. Jon simply used other substances during those times in his ongoing practice of self medicating.

Jon went to counseling with a gifted colleague of mine who, based upon our long standing friendship, served for free and came to love and know Jon better than anyone else. Jon would come home from his sessions filled with wonder and touched by the Spirit. Still he could not break free.

He broke away from the destructive girl friend and moved home. He dabbled with other relationships. He seemed to do better for awhile, but relapses always followed efforts at recovery. We were at our wits end.

He moved into his own apartment with another young woman whom he had known since high school. They were much in love and set up housekeeping together. Once again, the happiness was fleeting, soon devoured by Jon's rampant addiction and all the destructive behaviors that go with it. He lied to her. He used her. Things broke down and she asked him to move out. He moved home again, this time taking up residence in a basement room, with its own bath and ground level entrance.

About a month before Jon died, Jed, our golden retriever got so ill we had to arrange to have him euthanized. There is a veterinarian locally who will come to one's home in a working van and care for animals in all the needed ways. Jed had rapidly lost the use of his hind quarters and could not walk nor even perform the basic functions of life.

I made the call. Jean called Jon to come home. We together gave him a few tasty morsels to eat. Jed loved his "babies" which were his special stuffed chew toys. He loved to retrieve them with canine pride, and even slept with them in his mouth at times. This time Jon retrieved them for him and gave them to him for comfort.

The vet arrived. She was compassionate and kind. She did not hurry but worked smoothly and with tenderness. Jon and I held Jed as the vet administered, first one needle to sedate him and then a second, carrying the lethal dose of serum that sent him on his way out of this world. We had already dug the grave in the back yard. We tenderly loaded Jed on a cloth and carried him down and lowered him in.

We shoveled the dirt over him through many tears in our eyes. Our hearts were aching. As we walked back up the terrace steps together, I put my arm around Jon. I could feel his ribs, he'd become so skinny due to the drug abuse that totally messed up his ability to eat properly. I said, "Jon, this pain we're experiencing now is only one ten thousandth of the pain mom and I would feel if this ever happened to you. Please hold on, keep fighting and get better." He said, "I know, I was thinking the same thing." With care and love and his plumber's skill, Jon crafted a cross of copper pipe and placed it on Jed's grave. It is there to this day. One month later, the shoe finally dropped. Jon too was gone out of the world.

Chapter VI

The Night From Hell:
July 23rd, 2005

Jon seemed like he was going to make it. He was happy again, he had a new lady friend, and he had a new job with a landscaping company. It seemed like he'd taken to heart the adage of the recovery movement concerning people, places, and things. An addict cannot afford the luxury of being near anything or anyone, or to be anywhere that could trigger the old patterns of getting high.

One week before this terrible night, the family was all gathered in our family room. It was the night before our daughter Julia's wedding. Jon was to be the best man. Jon announced that he was going back to the plumbing company because the money was so much better and he couldn't see his way out of debt on the salary he was making as a landscaper. We all argued and begged him not to return. He assured us all that he knew what he was doing: he could "handle it".

The next day at the wedding, he looked gaunt, and in hindsight I remember that the joy was not in his countenance. On Monday, he started back plumbing. By Wednesday, it began to dawn on us that he was once again in serious trouble. On Friday evening, I was watching TV and Jon stopped to say hi. I asked if he was going out on a date. He said, "I wouldn't call it that." I said, "Take it easy." I was angry. I was frightened. I was mostly just worn out.

As a final interchange with my son it is not much on which to hang my heart. Few of us really know what will be our final chance to speak to someone we love. We take far too much for granted. We make way too many assumptions. We live as though we are entitled to more time, always more time. Within hours I would be disabused of all such notions.

In just a few minutes after Jean called 911 on that fateful night described above, we were surrounded and then moved aside by police and EMTs. They were kind and efficient. They knew what they could not say. Our son was dead. I could feel their pity fill the air.

O Lord, wake me up from this dream; put me to sleep somewhere far from this nightmare!

They strapped him to a back board, carried him out through the sliding door and loaded Jon into the ambulance. An officer offered to drive us to the nearby hospital. I opted to drive us myself, following a police car. It was now about 4 AM. As the police cruiser pulled away with us in tow, the neighbors on the corner had come out to watch and wonder what had come to pass. The pre-dawn darkness was sultry and eerily unreal. We wended our way through the deserted suburban streets. As a pastor, I'd traveled the same route to the same hospital to visit both family and friends on many occasions. The drive was never like this.

We approached the hospital, me driving on auto-pilot. I remember parking, walking, entering through the emergency entrance, waiting in the bright florescence of the ER lights, the knowing, sympathetic glances, the world weary faces that had seen it all too often, people who felt badly but who couldn't get in too deep. They would do their professional best and try to help ease us through this step in the emotional meat grinder of child loss.

"Mr. and Mrs.Gaskill, he's in room three; you may go in now." What do you do beside such an awful gurney? For me, it was way too early for tears. My face felt like a stone. My eyes sent my brain a message that I still had no way to comprehend. What was I looking at here? I had no way to know. I remember Jon's ankle socks covering his long feet and finger-like toes, his grey sweat pants, his tee shirt, his skinny and sallow visage displaying the ravages of drug addiction, and most prominent and poignant, the tattoo on his wrist, "resurrection". He'd been so proud of that ink. It was a statement, a declaration of freedom, of new life, of the Holy Spirit that his counselor Austin was helping him to discover. He wanted what we all so desperately wanted, prayed for, and dared to believe: Jon would beat the odds. Jon would get clean. Jon would live!

Jon was dead. Did the tattoo mock him and us in death? Or was it even on this night from hell a proclamation of the faith we all held dear, that life is stronger than death? I believe Lord, help thou my unbelief. The resurrection seemed a long way off, like a pinprick of light at the end of a very, very long tunnel.

Outside, the grey twilight was inching away from the dawn. Inside was still bright with artificial light, but there was no life. Jon lay stretched out, now a grey cadaver. He did not move. All was still. Occasionally, someone would slip in quietly to see if there was anything we needed, water for instance. What we needed we neither knew nor could they supply.

They seemed to need things from us. "I'm sorry Mr. Gaskill; I just need your signature on this form?" Various people, doctors, hospital staff, police confronted us with, "I'm sorry, I just need to ask you a few questions." Each had the official clipboard; each asked the same things, over and over. I began to get irritated. Why couldn't they just consult with one another instead of subjecting us to this grueling repetition of the horrid details of this night?

Should we stay? Should we go? There was no point in staying. I pried Jean away from that final room as gently as I could, knowing full well that this would be the last time we would ever lay eyes on our son in this world. There would be a cremation. There would be no viewing. There would be no cosmetic cover up through the undertaker's art. We walked past the sympathetic glances, and into the desolate dawn parking lot.

"We should make some calls, even though it's so early." Call son Mark, our oldest. No answer. Still asleep, no doubt. Call Julia. No answer. Call my sister Mary. No response. Call Steve, Jean's brother. Silence. Too early to call dear Aunt Fran. 6:01 AM. 6:02, 03, 12, 17, 29, 6:31 AM. Time crawled by at a snail's pace.

Around 7AM, a small red car pulled into the driveway. We stepped out to meet KT in the driveway. KT was Jon's new girlfriend with whom he hoped to be happy. They had planned when they said goodnight just hours earlier to go to Long Beach Island for a day of surfing. "I'm sorry KT, but Jon is gone. He died last night around 3 AM." "What?" Her incomprehension was complete. Then she dissolved in tears of shock and disbelief. Together we went inside.

I forget whom we reached first, but people finally began to answer the phone. We didn't know what to say to any who asked what we wanted them to do. Did we want them to come over? Did we want them to stay away for awhile? Ultimately, each person who heard would just have to make their own decisions. We were in no shape to manage the caregivers. Jean finally surrendered her natural tendency to circle her emotional wagons against intruders and submitted to the "come who may" flow of commiseration. Some asked permission; some simply arrived at the door. I don't remember now how the news spread like wildfire, but spread it did. Mary called Aunt Fran who was 93 at the time, a great lover of the Lord and of all of us. She wanted to come over, and of course the answer was yes.

The family began to gather. Jean's brother Steve and his wife Janet showed up. Church members sprang into action. Mounds of food began to arrive. And cards began to stream in a few days later. Flowers arrived in bunches. Neighbors on our street poured out concern, and some became a huge help. I arranged for another to preach for me on Sunday. My elders quickly met after that first service and told me to take as much time off as I needed, that they would cover the affairs of the church indefinitely.

One of Jon's drug buddies called. "Jon is dead! Don't ever call here again", I spit into the phone with hot anger and slammed the receiver down. Someone had to take the blame: drug buddies, people who had helped him score, people who had used him to help them score, his old girlfriend who had systematically undermined his self esteem and increased his need to medicate himself against the pain of living, all the enablers of this world, and possibly even me. Could I have been a better father? Is there something I could have done and didn't do? Could I have tried harder, shouted louder, prayed longer? And of course there was Jon himself. It all comes down to choices, and his had proved to be fatal.

Saturday rolled on to its sad conclusion and melted into Sunday morning. The day was passed, I don't remember how. We didn't know how to go on living, but we weren't dead, so we had to do so. Sunday evening fell, and I still hadn't heard from Jeff Brown, my friend and the funeral director whom I had asked the hospital to contact to remove Jon's body.

We had decided upon cremation and a memorial service for the following weekend. We decided that there were to be no obituaries in the paper in a vain attempt to exclude from our sorrow Jon's contacts from the drug infested world which he had foolishly inhabited. We hoped that all the public grieving would be done with before they ever found out. We were, I guess, trying to protect ourselves in some lame ways. It didn't work of course. They all knew within hours what had happened.

Finally I called Jeff, and discovered that the hospital had neglected to contact him. This explained why we hadn't heard from him as quickly as we expected. I think the real reason for the delay was that the autopsy had not yet been performed as it was the weekend and they simply put it off until they could get to it on Monday. Little snags like this add to the grief of bereaved people but our loss was so enormous that it didn't matter much at the time. Jeff assured me he would take care of Jon right away.

Chapter VII

Making Arrangements

On Tuesday, Jean agreed that I should go meet with Jeff to make final arrangements and select an urn for Jon's ashes. She had no desire to accompany me on the grim errand. On the drive over, I got a frantic call that my daughter Julia wanted to go with me on this mission and would I please swing by and pick her up? Of course I agreed.

We arrived. Jeff was helpful and kind. We paged through a catalogue of urns and selected one of oak with some engraving of trees on the front. I signed some forms, ordered some death certificates, told Jeff not to run obituaries in the local papers, and selected a prayer card. It was good to have a job to do. It was good to be, if just for a few minutes, a professional again, the minister working with the funeral director, tending to details, making sure and efficient decisions.

Then the wrench was tossed into the gears of this smoothly running little motor. Julia wanted to see him. Not a good idea. She became insistent. Jeff said it was not a good idea. She wanted to see him. So I had to tell her that an autopsy had been done. There had been no embalming and no cosmetic arts have been practiced here. What she would see would not be a healing memory. Please trust me. For once, she did and she relented. Our work was done and off we went. This was weird father and daughter time indeed.

Sometime later, we received the autopsy report. Jon had traces of several drugs in his blood. The killer was the cocaine that he injected directly into his arm. Jon had made a vow to himself not to use heroin again. "Stinkin' thinkin'" said that cocaine was not heroin; therefore it would not be a broken vow to test drive the ultimate high. Jon was a loser in a deadly game of chemical Russian roulette.

Chapter VIII

Witness to the resurrection: Worship From the Bottom of a Pit

O where have you been my blue eyed son?
And where have you been, my darling young one?
I've been out in front of a dozen dead oceans.
I've walked and I've crawled on six crooked highways.
I've been in the middle of seven sad forests.
I've been ten thousand miles in the mouth of a graveyard.
And it's a hard, it's a hard, it's a hard, it's a hard,
It's a hard rain's a gonna fall.

Bob Dylan

The week between Jon's death and the memorial service is mostly a blur to me now. Friends and family gathered around us. People we hadn't seen or heard from in some time made contact. Cards poured in. We had so much food we had to give some away. Friends John and Linda, along with Al and Nancy came from New Hampshire and Randy and Donna came up from Virginia. They gathered for much needed love and support.

I began to plan the service. I asked John, my longtime friend from seminary days to participate with readings and prayers.

Randy, my partner in ministry and in prayer for many years, agreed to help as well. I called Austin to see if he would preach.

Austin and I came from the same home church in Narberth, Pa. back in the mid-seventies. Austin grew up Roman Catholic on the streets of South Philadelphia but by some weird twist of predestination he became a Presbyterian. He was a fiery, red-headed Irishman. Now he is bald with gray sidewalls, and still just as fiery! His life is unconventional and he is intense, about the Lord and about life.

Austin had freely counseled with Jon for about a year prior to his death. He had a level of intensity that Jon was stunned to discover. He would return from his counseling times spiritu-ally energized and deeply touched. Something was happening inside of Jon's heart as a result of these sessions. Austin got deep inside of Jon, and, as it turned out, Jon got deep inside of Austin as well.

I came to believe that Austin knew Jon better than anyone else, maybe even better than I did. I was so grateful for another to make contact with my son and to hold out the hope and power of our faith. I was thankful for another whom I count as a brother in Christ who had the generosity and the courage to step beyond the professional boundaries of counselor/client roles and meet my son heart to heart, faith to faith, and man of God to man finding God. Of course there was friction between the tectonic plates in the soul of one who was both seeker and addict. Every gain was met with a commensurate defeat and the drugs asserted their mastery over Jon's life again and again. Earthquakes of the Spirit were met with persistent aftershocks of addiction.

For years, I have been the family preacher, conducting wed-dings, administering the Sacrament of Baptism, and preaching the funerals of relatives far and near. I preached at both of my parents' funerals. I wouldn't have had it any other way. But this was a funeral I had no business conducting, and thank God I knew it.

Preaching the funerals of loved ones contorts the grieving process. Everyone else makes a beginning while you are working. There is usually a tiny fissure between leading worship and worship itself. Once in a while, the gap is bridged and worship leadership melds into unbridled worship for the leader as well as the people. But this seamlessness is not a given.

Spirit filled worship is fluid and dynamic. It flows in a direction determined by the Spirit. Worship leaders collaborate with the Spirit to help lead the people along in the direction appointed by the Spirit. The attentiveness and focus required in leading worship upon the death of a loved one delays and even subverts the grieving of the preacher subtly and sometimes significantly. One must stay focused upon the task of leading others into the presence of the Lord. It is worship in God's presence that carries the healing of God into each human heart. It is all too easy to be consumed by the responsibilities of such leadership and end up missing your own healing encounter in the process.

I would have no such distractions with my son. So Austin agreed to pay the price. I will never forget the value of this gift of love given to me and my family and to Jon. Austin shared with me sometime later how thoroughly spent he was for a season after this experience. He left a huge chunk of his own soul on the table in that one passionate act of preaching and leading worship.

During the week, Julia and Jon's friends gathered at her apartment to make several collages of photos of Jon's life. It was grief therapy 101. They selected photos and relived some of the stories behind them. They laughed. They cried. They did a beautiful job. The poster boards were on display at the memorial service, and then stood in our living room for over a year.

I selected a program cover for the service of witness to the resurrection. On the front, there was a picture of a light house and the following words were printed:

"When we become Christians we become keepers of the light of Christ. Occasionally one of us may be asked to do something dramatic to save another-some daring or life-changing effort that will pluck another person from danger. But most of us will help save lives for Christ by being faithful in the daily routines; by using everyday tasks to show other people what a life with Him can be-by always forgiving and always loving; by holding the hands of those grieving. If we love one another in the name of Jesus, no doubt we will help   save lives."

I call this the ministry of mustard seeds and leaven; it is in the little, often unseen acts of kindness that the hearts of the bereaved are most blessed and carried along.

And this verse of scripture was also on the cover:

"Shine as lights in the world; holding forth the word of life." Philippians 2:15-16.

I worked to plan the service, picking scriptures and hymns. I determined to play a few songs on guitar as a prelude. I was not going to preach but I felt compelled to offer some parting gift of love to Jon. Mark expressed the desire to join me, so we sang two songs together, several verses of "A Hard Rain's Gonna Fall," by Bob Dylan, and the old gospel song, "I'll Fly Away." Then I sang two alone, one of which was, "I Can Only Imagine":

I can only imagine, what it will be like
When I walk by your side
I can only imagine when all I will do
Is forever, forever worship you
I can only imagine

Surrounded by your glory what will my heart feel?
Will I dance for you Jesus or in awe of you be still?
Will I stand in your presence or to my knees will I fall?
Will I sing hallelujah; will I be able to speak at all?
I can only imagine. I can only imagine.
                                                    Bart Millard

As is usually the case when a young person dies, there were hundreds of people who turned out. There were many that I didn't know. There were many that didn't know Jon but who came to support Jean and me and the family. There were cousins and relatives not seen in a long time as well. The sheer magnitude of the crowd was a comfort.

The congregation sang, "What a Friend We Have in Jesus," and read together Psalm 130: "Out of the depths I cry to Thee, O Lord! Lord, hear my voice!" We prayed. Other scriptures were read. We sang. We cried and clung to one another. My three close friends, Randy, John, and Austin led the worship. My choir director and dear friend Leon DeLoach sang a solo of "Just As I Am."

Austin preached a heart wrenching and passionate sermon entitled "The Silent Prophet" which was filled with love, urgency, and with an intensity that was almost frightening to some. He spoke of the spiritual warfare that surrounds each life. He spoke deeply and insightfully of Jon, revealing much about the deep and tender heart that lay buried under the addiction. The message was just at the fervent level that I needed it to be, no matter what others might have thought about it. Austin had taken Jon into his own heart at a level beyond professionalism, not short of it. His insight into the soul of my son was true comfort to me.

The final hymn sung was, "For All the Saints." The lyrics to these stanzas of this great hymn are particularly poignant:

For all the saints, who from their labors rest, Who Thee by faith before the world confessed, Thy name, O Jesus, be forever blessed: Alleluia! Alleluia!

Thou wast their rock, their fortress, and their might, Thou, Lord, their captain in the well fought fight; Thou in the darkness drear, their one true Light: Alleluia! Alleluia!

From earth's wide bounds, from ocean's farthest coast,
Thru gates of pearl streams in the countless host, Singing
to Father, Son, and Holy Ghost: Alleluia! Alleluia!

Text by William W. How

On the back page of the program, we included several entries from the prayer journal of Jon's great aunt Fran Corey, my mother's older sister. Words that appeared in italics came as promptings from God's Spirit, while Fran's prayers were in normal type.

Entry from July 13, ten days before Jon's death: *"Don't give up on Jon; I haven't and never will. I'm claiming him for my kingdom, soon and very soon."*

Entries from the morning of July 23rd, when the news about Jon came:

Dear One, I come. Please speak to our aching hearts today, Lord. Was this what you meant Lord, "soon and very soon", that you were claiming him for your kingdom? Please don't let me miss what you would say now.

"Frances, don't ever doubt that you hear me. I love you! I love the whole family. I don't send more than you can bear. Remember, all things work together for good to those who are called according to my purpose. You are- all of you. Take my peace." About 10:30 AM.

"Jon is here with me. He's sorry. Here he can grow faster." At noon.

"Let me have him." 12:45 PM.

The day of the funeral rolled on into numbness. Refreshments in the church parlor following the service gave way to the gathering of close family and friends at our home. In the days ahead, a river of sympathy cards would begin to arrive. Visitors came and went. The phone rang with calls from well-wishers. We were loved and supported by so many people it was humbling and mostly helpful. We were so thankful for the thoughtfulness of the people around us. We were also exhausted.

Chapter IX

Helpful Condolences

I just spent several hours looking through the cards we received which number, I'm guessing without counting them, about two hundred. I sat down to read them in one sitting, this nearly four years later. It was emotionally exhausting. Some were fancy, some plain, some with short notes, a few with devotional articles or clippings of one kind or another, some just signed by name, and a few from neighboring congregations that had several hundred signatures on them. "You are in our thoughts and prayers at this difficult time," was the most common note. Or, "Words cannot express how we feel about you in your loss."

Every card or note represented someone who thought enough to send some love, to make some contact, to try to help us feel not so alone. Several people sent multiple cards over a period of months, and I remember that the farther removed in time they were, the more they meant. The ones that came from parents who had lost a child themselves carried special weight. I received cards from parishioners from the church I served for sixteen years in Pennsylvania and from my current congregation. Several recalled how my ministry had helped them at their times of loss or struggle and how they wished they could return the favor now.

A card is a simple thing. Sending one to the bereaved is an important way to give small doses of comfort. I pulled out a few notable samples from the pile that I found to be particularly meaningful because the people had obviously made a real effort to communicate at a deeper level. I share some excerpts below to show the sort of sentiments that I found helpful in case you ever have to walk with a friend through this kind of tragedy.

Dear Bill and Jean, There are no words to express how sorry I was to hear of Jonathan's death and your loss. When our children are born, we have such hopes and dreams. Their smiles and tears, their warm breath on our neck as we cuddle them are all so special. And as they grow, the first day of school, the first lost tooth, the first solo bike ride and the first best friend are happy memories. But then they grow up and parents and family are relegated to the background. Friends and acceptance take precedence. We do all we can. We give them all our love, but sometimes that is still not enough. While they are trying to find themselves, other temptations lead them astray and sometimes they never find their way back. Love Jonathan; grieve for Jonathan, but God will give you the strength to allow the nightmare to fade and the happy memories to remain. Please know that my thoughts and prayers are with you both. I don't want to intrude on your grieving but if I can be of any help, please let me know. Yours in Christ, Sue K.

From a parishioner who lost a son some years before I arrived as pastor:

Dear Jean and Bill, I was on vacation in Maine when Jonathan died and just learned of the very sad news last night. I know of the ache in your hearts and how hard it is to face each day without him. I got consolation knowing "there's a time to be born and a time to die," and I hope you too can feel that. Some days you'll wonder how other friends can be having such a good time when your heart is breaking, or a certain song will bring on the tears, but some day you'll be able to smile again. With love, Marge M.

From a church member who is also a dear friend:

Dearest Jean, There's not a minute of any day that you are not in my thoughts, held up in prayer. There's an ache in my heart that's with me all the time, trying to imagine, unable to imagine, what this must be like for you. I want so much just to sit with you and hold you, one mother to another, or help you with some of the hard tasks ahead. But I suspect that your greatest need right now may be just to close ranks with your family and have some quiet time alone together. I will call you in a few days just to check in. If you want some company, I'm glad to offer that; if you want some space, I'm glad to give that too. In either case, just know that I love you. J.

From a young parishioner:

I'm really sorry about your son. I remembered that I still had the coin that you gave me after his surfing trip (I had given some coins from Tonga out during a children's message), and I thought you might want to have it. Also, here is a coin from my collection for you. (a small coin with a cross cut out of the center; both coins were taped inside the card). Love you, Payton W.

This from a young woman, a parishioner and friend of Jon's:

Dear Jean and Bill, I don't even know how to begin to say all the things I want to convey. Your family is a 2ⁿᵈ family to me and I love you all very much. This is a difficult time for all of us, but you most of all. Knowing he is in a better place is the only thing that makes missing him bearable. He can finally be completely happy. And yet the rest of us are still here finding our way without him. Jon taught me so much about life and not letting a day go by without truly living it. I know it's not easy, by any means, but I want you to know I'm here for you. I was reading a devotion on Malachi 3:3 the other day and thought of you. It was talking about how the silversmith refines the silver by holding it in the hottest part of the fire and if he takes his gaze off of it, even for a moment, it could burn up and be destroyed. Jon's death is a part of the fire that is refining us all. In the end I hope the Great Refiner sees his reflection more clearly in me and in you because of it. In the past couple of months since Jon's death I have seen a change in many people and I know that there is a change in me and my daily outlook. Jon always said to not let a day go by without living it. Even before he found the Tim McGraw song ("Live Like You Were Dying"), he lived his life that way. I love you both! J.

From parents of Steve, one of Jon's closest friends who also lost a young son:

Dear Bill and Jean, Please accept our deepest condolences and prayers for Jonathan and for your family. You have lost a loving son and the world has lost a great promise. Jonathan has been a dear friend to our family for many years and his presence is deeply missed. When we lost our son, we felt great sadness and a grief that we continue to live with. Like your Jonathan, our son left us too early. Please be comforted by the knowledge that we believe it's not the amount of time one lives, but it's how one loves that determines a life's value. After all, our lives are but a flash of a moment in eternity! Jon was like a brother to Stephen (their surviving youngest son) when Stephen needed him the most. Jon will be greatly missed. We take comfort in the knowledge that he is now safe in God's arms. May God bless you, Chuck and Lorraine C.

From a dear friend, Nancy:

Several weeks ago, my dear friend Judy J. and I gathered for prayer at her home. Before we began, she showed me her bedroom which she had never before allowed me to see. She has over the past three months been in the process of painting her walls, picking up the clutter, and carpeting her floors. Their bedroom was where their precious daughter, Jill, passed into eternity after her battle with cancer. As she shared with me, I fell into her arms and we sobbed together for you and for her as she was approaching the 8th anniversary of her daughter's death. As I asked her "will my friends ever be ok?" she answered me that you would be in time. That afternoon Judy phoned to say she was cleaning in her art room and found a note card she had designed and asked if I would I like to send it to my friends? I told her that would be wonderful as I am trying to send cards regularly and this would probably be special as Judy certainly understands your pain in a way I cannot. I pray that in God's economy, the pain Al and I and others feel for you will somehow relieve some of yours. We love you so very much, Al and Nancy L.

Finally, this letter from my son Mark to my sister Mary and her husband, Larry:

Dear Aunt May May and Uncle Larry, It seems like a long time ago that you handed me several bags containing presents for every holiday in the remaining calendar year. I thank you for the birthday gift and your thoughtfulness. When we left New Jersey after Julia's wedding, I never would have guessed what the next few weeks would hold for our family. I would like to tell you that I know how much your presence and your help have meant to Mom and Dad in the past weeks. Even though both of you are certainly grieving, you have been able to provide strength and comfort to Mom, Dad, Julie, and me. It does mean a great deal to have family around in such a time.

Jonathan's passing has left a void in our family, a voice has been silenced; a presence has been taken away. No doubt for a very long time we will sense what Jim Loder called "the presence of an absence." But it will fade, it will be filled by new additions, new events, life will go on. Even now as I am engaged in our church's Bible school program I find that there is freedom from the constant thought of a lost brother. As I lead groups of children singing songs of praise with Jon's guitar, I come to appreciate the sentimental weight of something that was left behind. And I think of how appropriate it is to use the guitar as an instrument of worship, bringing glory to the name of God who now holds Jon in his care.

It was strange to look over his things and pick out what "I wanted." My first thought was that I didn't really "want" anything, not this way. But as I played his guitar with my Dad, I thought about how many of the last times I spent with Jon were teaching him to play certain songs. Our memories are so often bound up in things. Of course Jon himself is no longer bound up in things or by things, or by ideas. Jon now lives in the pure light of heaven, growing in God's presence. Aunt Fran's prayer journal obviously resonates in my mind, the part about him growing but also the final command: "Let me have him." It is what we all must do, we must let go, we must move on with life. Through the sadness, as we sort through things, memories and thoughts, we must trust that God now has complete control of Jon's life and is doing what must be done to bring into being a new creation.

Thanks again for the gift and all that you have done in recent weeks. We love you and thank God for your presence with us in this time. Love, Mark

Chapter X

The Beginning of the Hangover

May 1st, 2009 As I awoke this morning, the thought came to me that not only did Jon live like he was dying, he was dying while he was living, which is true of all of us in one sense. But watching drugs steal his life right before my eyes was like dealing with a slow death that was moving inexorably toward its conclusion. So the grief began long before the fateful night that he died. The dying had been going on for some time. I mentioned the emptiness that people feel when they lose a loved one in a recent sermon. A dear woman who has been gradually losing her husband to dementia greeted me at the door after worship and said that some like her experience the losses while their loved ones are still alive. I know exactly what she meant. It is a painful and poignant insight.

First Year Prayers:

Dear Lord, I am like a wounded dog in the corner. I need care but I am withdrawn into my pain and my defenses. I dare not let any come close lest they deepen the gashes I have upon my soul. I would cry out to you, but my prayers simply mock me as they rise into a silent and darkened sky. I still have my faith. My core convictions remain strong. But I fear that my cries have drowned out your still small voice. I have known our relationship through prayer in the past to be very much a two way conversation. You have heard my voice, and I have heard yours. Now the only voice I hear is my own. I am rubbed raw by the constant grief that engulfs me by day and awakens me by night to engulf me again. Lord, hear my cry. Don't throw me away because my trust is so battered and bruised. I know that by your mercy I may one day trust you and your goodness once again. Lord have mercy. Christ have mercy. Lord have mercy upon me. Amen

Good morning God. I awake against all desire, but sleep is short and fleeting. My bed is bathed in sadness night after long night. I lay awake beside my beloved wife and feel a palpable grief hanging like an evil aura over our insomniac bodies. I hunger for hope for a brighter tomorrow but find none. I yearn for comfort and receive it in doses far too small for the size of my sorrow. The sadness feels like a huge, immovable boulder lying on my chest and making it hard to breathe. I am calling to you out of the darkness, you who are the light of the world. Shed some light in my direction that I may once again know for sure that you love me and Jean. Cast us not away from your presence and take not your Holy Spirit from us. Restore to us the joy of your salvation and uphold us by the power of your Spirit. We sit mired in sorrow awaiting your rescue to come. Help Lord! We desperately need you. Amen.

God, this lonely grief is numbing. I've lost my capacity to care about the normal things that concern most people. They have lost all importance to me. I fear that I will slide into a sloth from which I will never emerge. Deliver me from this living Sheol, this place of shadows, this land behind your back. Direct me to the land of the living some day and don't let me go down to the pit, never to return. Fix your eyes upon me and turn your face toward me. I am in deep distress. Hasten to help me I pray, in Jesus' name. Amen.

Lord Jesus, I come to you because you too were a man of sorrows, well acquainted with grief. I need to know that you feel the same indignation for Jon's death that you expressed at the tomb of your dear friend Lazarus. I need to know that my loss makes you once again deeply moved and troubled in spirit. I need to know that even now you weep. I need my sorrow to be absorbed in your divine sorrow. I don't think I can bear it alone. It is a crushing weight upon my heart. Lord, hear my prayer and be swift to my side. For mercy's sake, look upon me, and all who are heart broken, with your compassion. Amen.

Jesus. I cry for help but there is none that can reach me. I am like a lonely bird in a wilderness with no food or water in sight. There is just the parching sun and arid wind of sadness that saps my soul and my strength. I worship you from a dry and thirsty land. I try to pray, but the sound of my own voice seems to mock me: "Why speak into the void with futile words? Why not keep your peace and suffer like a man? You are nothing but alone. No help is on the way. No one hears and no one cares. Listen, all around you are the sounds of sorrow. Your wife grieves for her son, your son and daughter for their brother. What help has come to them?" Be silent, O despair. Be silent, O my enemy. God will yet hear my cry and help me and us all, for Jesus' sake. It is in His name, the faithful name that I pray. Amen.

Chapter XI

If There's Anything I Can Do to Help

One of the well intended offers people make when hard times strike is, "If there's anything I can do, please call." Or they say, "If you need anything, just call." They are saying, "I care," or "I feel helpless," or "I want you to know I'm thinking of you," or some variation of noble sentiments. I've done the same thing too many times to count.

But what sufferers know is that such offers are rarely very helpful, not because they are ill intended but because people in grief are unable to take them up on the offer. Someone in the degree of pain that child loss brings can no more call up and ask for assistance than they could walk on water. We can't make that call. We don't know what we need or what would help. We don't want to be alone but we don't want to impose. Our pain is intensely personal and even private. We would like to be able to share it, to siphon off its crushing intensity, but we can't do it. The grief is so intense that it is wild and out of control. We are frightened by it. We have no idea where it will take us or how long it will last. We are afraid of you all, that you will say something well intended but not wise that will deepen the pain we are already enduring. We are afraid you will come near and we will be hurt. We are afraid you will read our signals and you will stay away and leave us even more desolate than we are already. We don't trust anyone who has never been where we are standing right now except for a few others who have earned our trust over the years in other less intense situations.

We need concrete offers, especially in the first few days and weeks following our loss. One such offer was made by my brother-in-law, Larry. Larry has been a rock in our family. A retired colonel who served in the Army in many places including Korea, Vietnam, and Central America, as well as locations in the States from the deep South, where he was raised, to Manhattan in New York. He served as vice president in charge of security at the Federal Reserve Bank in Philadelphia following retirement from the military. It was there that he met my sister Mary and married her shortly thereafter.

Jon had run up large debts to creditors, in addition to those he managed to cajole his way into on our credit cards. Like most addicts, Jon became adept at getting what he wanted and what he was convinced he needed. It was not just drugs. It was a motorcycle here, a new truck there, another surf board over here, even furniture and a big screen TV for his girlfriend's mother. He emulated the Godfather, which was one of his favorite movies. It was tongue in cheek mostly, but not totally.

By the time Jon died, we had already become tormented to the point of exasperation by the threatening letters from bill collectors and the countless times each day our phone rang with pleas and threats from Jon's collection of creditors. It took us several years just to pay off the debt that had accrued to us due to Jon's charming hustle of his too soft parents.

Larry knew of our plight and offered to handle all the outside creditors. Talk about a gift! This was more helpful than all the vague offers of support rolled into one. Every time I got a letter, I'd hand it over to Larry and he would call the company in question, explain the circumstances and that there were no assets and there was no estate. He persuaded each one, one by tedious one, to relent and write off Jon's bad debts.

I felt no remorse on this front because I believed then, and still believe, that the offer of easy credit has gotten more than a few of our youth into deep financial troubles long before they've gained the maturity to use credit wisely. Larry waded through this muck of Jon's debt tirelessly until every last letter and call ceased to come. The concreteness of his offer and the faithfulness that he showed in persisting to the end stands in my mind as a shining example of how to really help the bereaved.

Of course not all gifts of help are so extravagant, nor do they need to be. Some just dropped by to visit and listen. One lady who had lost three husbands and two sons, one son to drugs and another shortly thereafter in a car accident, let us use her cottage on Long Beach Island. Others took us out to dinner. Others sent cards months later. Others would discreetly ask about our welfare. Others sent money. All of it was unsolicited, for as I said, we didn't know what to ask for or how to ask even when we did know our need. Many, like my sister Mary and my dear Aunt Fran simply prayed for us, that great intangible gift that is impossible to measure, but which intuitively I sensed was doing much to carry us along in what became a sheer struggle for survival. Both also sent numerous cards over the course of many months, a gentle reminder that our grieving had not been forgotten.

A valuable gift has been given annually by my brother-in-law Steve and his wife Janet who have had Thanksgiving dinner for all the family at their home in West Chester, Pa. We used to have the feast at our home much of the time. Thanksgiving had become a "reminder day." We used to be reminded of warm memories past, but since Jon's death it had become a reminder of recent dashed hopes. We would hope for a day of rest and togetherness and thankfulness. What we would get would be memories of Jon rolling in late, and then slipping off to get stoned or to meet one of his women, and presumably get high. Or we would recall how he would be high already by the time we all got together and how he would slump on a sofa somewhere in a stupor. Steve and Janet provided a welcome change of venue that has been so helpful in enabling us reclaim the warmth of one holiday at least.

In addition to those who offer concrete and tangible aid, the other important comforters come in two categories: those who have also lost children themselves, and those who have learned to merely listen and be present, especially those who will listen and be present over the long haul, who will suffer to hear the story of our arduous journey over and over, even long after the flowers have wilted and died and the stream of sympathy cards has dried up. As one friend said to me as we walked several years later down a country road in northern New Hampshire, you gradually lose permission from people to speak of your loss the more time that goes by. People no longer expect, and some may not even welcome, us bringing up of the subject of our sorrow.

Chapter XII

Flat Lining

"O yeah, life goes on, long after the thrill of livin' is gone."

John Mellencamp

Journal entry: August, a few weeks after the funeral. On Long Beach Island at a cottage graciously given by a friend who also lost two children and three mates.

Jon is gone. Dead? No. Not living here anymore. Those of us who are left are not living here anymore either, not the way we used to live. Now, we inhabit that grieving land, a land of grayness, shadows, and isolation one from another. I see my beloved, across the room, across the Grand Canyon. Sorrow and anger shimmer in the air between us. Mornings are hard. So are mid-days and so are sundowns. And sleep? It comes when it must, but it does its dirty work of transporting us to another painful sunrise.

Time stood still like lead at first. Now it creeps by, going seemingly nowhere in pointless direction. My youngest son, father of my sorrows, progenitor of my inconsolable wife, your own mother bereft of her baby boy, her joy and crown, gone.

Would be comforters are many at first. When they are most eager to help, when the grief is raw and new, is when we are least able to accept it. When we are more ready, they'll have moved on I suspect, figuring that the worst, which has just begun, is now over.

We sail on into uncharted waters. Many others have been here before us, but can leave only hints and clues, but no maps. What it was for you it will not be for me. Each of us will bear our own load, mostly alone. Those who too have lost a child are within hailing distance at least.

Very quickly in the first few days, guilt demons had to be dispatched to the pit or the lake of fire where they belong. Who's to blame? He? We? You? They? The world, the flesh, the devil, God? All of the above? None of the above? It's a fruitless pursuit trying to find someone or something to pin it on. He's gone. Can you explain it, how or why? He's still gone. Could you have done more? Could I, we, or they? Could this have been prevented? Questions of the mind that is restless and demanding: "Satisfy me or else!" Or else what? Or else nothing. Empty promises (as though reasons could heal the heart), and empty threats, (as though failure to explain could make matters worse).

I told Jean I feared she'd become so consumed with grief that there would be no room for me anymore. She cries, she has no hope or enthusiasm for life. Grief! I dread this sorrow. I know it won't move out easily or soon. I know it will show up at all the times of tradition and celebration: Thanksgiving, Christmas, birthdays, family gatherings, and unexpectedly at many an in- between time. The presence of an absence.

Julia comes by to say goodbye to Mark. Two on the sofa, one missing: gone. Logan (grandson) chirping for his uncle Jon. Godfather. "Um babba" (Jon's nonsensical self designation), Jon's grin from the pictorial collages in the living room, left over from the funeral. His smile-less pose. His haunted eyes. His drug drained soul. Proud papa (me) cradling my infant son (him) on a shirtless summer day.

How shall I go on? How return to preach? Why should I take time off? My parishioners had no such luxury when their children died. They just went on in mute agony. Will they now resent me for coddling myself, these tough minded grievers? Will the spirit of jealousy now bite me? Or will they be tolerant for my sake and wish me well?

Journal entry, 5 AM, the second morning at Long Beach Island, date unknown. I've lost track of time. It's been a beastly hot summer. I try not to complain.

Most nights I wake up several times. 3 AM: "This is about when Jean began to lay awake that night. Am I still tired? Am I rested enough to get up? What time did I go to bed?" 3:55 AM: "This is when she found him. I hear over again her terrified call up to me, "Jon's OD'd" Shall I get up now? It's definitely late enough to get up. 5 AM: That's it; I can't fight it any more. I'm up.

Usually I shower first thing. Not this morning since I'm at the beach. I love the early morning. It's so quiet. Of course, on 7/23, we were enroute to the hospital for the formalities of pronouncing Jon gone. We endured the same interviews, the same questions over and over. The people were nice enough, but it just got to be too much. "Talk to each other, dammit! Compare notes. My wife and I are numb with loss. Let us go!" Go where? Home. Where is that now?

Our bedroom here in Mona's cottage has large windows facing the bay. We had a beautiful thunder and lightning storm last night, with pounding rain on the roof. I loved it, but was tired enough not to rise and watch. I slept soundly between the awakenings which haunt most every night.

Yesterday on the beach was sad. I was invisibly sorrowing. I felt like my face should have exuded such pain that people would part like the Red Sea as I walked among them. But none even noticed of course. My mind's eye saw Jon everywhere, at all ages, from sand castles and sand crabs, to skim boards to surf boards. Here he is now, Mr. Adonis in a wet suit, surf board under one arm, checking the waves. "I know you're looking, longing ladies, checking me out, but I must be about my more important work of wave riding. There'll be time for you later." As my dear friend John said of Jon in his trademark Armenian falsetto as he observed him at his brother Mark's wedding reception, "He's so cool!" The coolest cat on the beach, always.

I saw fathers with their video camcorders, catching their kids on the waves. Part of me said, "Good idea!", but I felt, "What does it matter. If you lose them, you won't want to watch those films." We have a few films of Jon but right now I have no desire to watch them, indeed I don't know if I could. Everyone says I should. Maybe later. Maybe.

At this point in my journal, there are several paragraphs dealing with contacts, either by visit or by card or by phone from people that either I had disappointed or had somehow betrayed me in the past. Most of their efforts were not helpful now. I found myself feeling mistrustful of their motives and wrestling with suspicion. Some were puzzling. Others made me angry. Broken relationships were still broken even when the tragedy of death strikes and these misguided attempts to touch us did not restore those damaged friendships. Without prior reconciliation, the giving of help is not possible.

There would be more disappointments in the coming months from people I thought would be there for me but who disappeared like a mist on an August morning. Several friends that I considered to be fairly close receded into a distant silence. This increased our pain and isolation. We were left to wonder if we had offended them in some way. In our overwhelming grief did we say something that drove them away? Were they having problems of their own which left no time or energy for us? Were we so frightening in our sorrow that they could not bear to come near?

I asked God what to make of all this and I heard something like, "You are not to turn any of this away. Accept it. Don't try to judge it or interpret it. The issues with all are best now left with me. Focus on life and grace, not old hurts. There is more than enough bitterness and hurt in the world already. Don't add to it."

I decided that I would not assume responsibility to care for the care-givers. I told myself that if I could not get a pass for something I said or something I neglected to do in this situation that those who deserted me were friends I could learn to live without. Some later tried to resume contact but their attempts seemed superficial and insincere so I put them off. I forgave them because I did not want to carry the added burden of bitterness which would only gnaw at the inner recesses of my own soul and I was already tattered and torn enough inside. The best I could do at the time was to wish them as well as I could, then just let them go.

The journal continues:

Mona's husband, Bill S., died on Jon's birthday, April 10ᵗʰ of this year, so her own grief is young. I started that evening at Charlie C's retirement party, which was just getting going when I made my excuses to go be with Jon and friends at a spur of the moment birthday party instigated by Julia at Kaminski's Pub. Jon turned twenty-four in the midst of the anorexic after shock period following the surgical insertion of a narcotic suppressing pellet in his arm designed to provide a period for de-tox. I stopped home on the way and there was a message from Mona's friend to go the hospital as soon as possible. Her husband Bill was not doing well. Within minutes of my arrival at the hospital and greeting Mona and Bill's two sons, he took his last peaceful breath and passed into eternity.

I've been on hand for the last breath of several people in my years of ministry. The experience has always been one of deep peacefulness. Mona and her sons were so glad I had come and I too was glad. I almost didn't come at once because of Jon's party. After prayers with Mona and her family, I took my leave.

So then, back to Kaminski's I went. Jon was in his element. I don't remember all the friends who came. There was a live musician taking requests in the corner of the pub. Jon made numerous requests, all of which the guitarist sang and played. Jon danced with Jean, probably to "Earth Angel" but I don't remember for certain. Jon adored his mom! And he requested Neil Young's, "The Needle and the Damage Done."

I caught you knocking at my cellar door
I love you baby can I have some more
Oh, oh, the damage done.

I hit the city and I lost my band
I watched the needle take another man
Gone, gone, the damage done

I sing the song because I love the man
I know that some of you don't understand
Milk-blood to keep from running out

I've seen the needle and the damage done
A little part of it in every one
O, Oh, the damage done

I've seen the needle and the damage done
A little part of it in every one
But every junkie's like a setting sun

Neil Young

This song was to become my own personal grief anthem in the near future. I played and sang it hundreds of times, to myself alone, in the time after Jon's death. I played and cried, played and cried. I tried to play it softly, out of ear shot of Jean for I knew it would not help her sorrow to hear such a grim anthem.

Going through his papers the Sunday after he died, I found the lyrics to "Damage Done" in his writing with "attention Dad" next to the title. He wanted me to teach it to him on guitar. Maybe he wanted to alert me. It didn't feel like a cry for help, but who knows. I missed much as a dad. Maybe if I'd been more aggressive, less passive, etc., etc., etc. The path of self-recrimination is a dark rabbit hole I chose not to run down. I was looking at Jon's written out lyrics to "Damage Done" and in

typical Jon phonics he had written "every junkie's like a setting
son*." O my!*

*So here I am on Long Beach Island. There's no hole in the
ground. Just the vast Atlantic Ocean stretching out far over
the horizon, which one day hence will passively receive Jon's
ashes. Earth to earth, ashes to ashes, dust to dust, surfer to
waves. And gone.*

Chapter XIII

Growing Through Agony

*A*ugust 7th. Other deaths, deaths in old age and fullness of years, end what is, what has been. Jon's death has raided the future. What might have been will never be. Hope is future- oriented; therefore in death hope takes a serious hit, especially when the victim is young. The despair rushes in with her sisters, cynicism, pessimism, and hopelessness. Faith says, "You won't have 'that' future, but you will have 'a' future. The future we had hoped for is radically different than the one that waits. It's a future we're not even sure we want. The future coming now is one that doesn't include Jon in the way we had hoped. We had hoped he would recover, win, get straight and clean, prosper, marry, father children, and be with us when we grew old. Gone! All gone! The word keeps recurring, pounding in my brain. Gone.*

Gone.
  The anger rooted in fear,
    In the feelings of being disrespected
      Disregarded
      Ignored

Gone.
    The chance to make all things right,
        To make all things new
        To take back what I said
        To say the things I should
Gone

        The chance to become the father that I would,
        given another chance
        The chance for you to become the son beyond
        The confusion and struggle of your youth
Gone

    We almost made it, man to man. You and me.
    Was I asking, expecting, demanding too much?
    Did I give you far too little of myself? Now you are;
    gone.
Gone
    The struggle to keep you alive.
        To make you see
        To help you understand
Gone
    Your mischievous vigor for life and for adventure
    Your courage and your cowardice
    Your fragility and your strength
Gone
    My youngest son is gone. He will not return to me,
    But I will go to him.
Gone
    the chasm between us, the dark void,
    The veil that interloped on earth.

Gone

Monday, August 8th. I woke up reliving the death scene, the 911 call, the verdict: he's gone. We all seem to share the growing conviction that Jon was heading rapidly down the rat hole of addiction, and that bad things were in store for him and for us. So, his passing was a severe mercy? Passing? You mean death! Shall I now engage in euphemisms to soften the blow? Not yet, please, not ever if I can avoid it.

Mona left Mitch Albom's, <u>Five People You Meet in Heaven</u>, which Jean and I both read. It was mostly good and comforted Jean especially, if just briefly. One fights for moments of respite. It dealt with sin, guilt, forgiveness, relationships and the inter-connections of the stories of the human family. No life is point-less. So what was the point of Jon's life? I couldn't even begin to say. I'd only have my view. So what was his point to me? This is a little scary! Let me try.

Jonathan: the name means God has given. Jon was a sur-prise baby. We weren't sure about a third child. I already felt stretched with two children, but Jean wanted another girl in the worst way. She quickly accepted him, all boy, and we loved him from birth. We took delight in him. I never have thought of my kids as having either point or purpose that needed definition. I just loved them in their own right as people whom God intended to live and whom I would love and for whom I would do my best. My "best" doesn't seem very good at this moment, but I will fight against going down the dead end street of self-recrimination.

Prayer: Oh Lord, you made me. You remember that I am dust. Made from dust. Returning to dust. Who am I that now I lay beaten and bloody in the ditch? Who am I that you should be my neighbor, turn aside, bind up my wounds and see to my care? The real question, the theological question is, "Who are you?" **I am. Being. Life. Love itself.** *All points and purposes emanate from you. I understand your answer to Job now more than ever. You blew him away. It was enough. Amen.*

> *Grief.*
>> *Guilt. Blame.*
>>> *Meaning. Purpose.*
>>>> *Forgiveness. Comfort.*
>>>>> *Hopelessness. Despair.*
>>>>>> *Black hole. Empty future.*
>>>>>>> *Tortured now.*
>>>>>> *Time empty, standing still at first,*

Then creeping along. To what end?
Grief.
Isolated and alone.
Rachel weeping for her children,
refusing to be comforted,
For they are no more.

What of the others? I have, still alive, Mark and Julia. They need to know that our love for them has not ended in our grief for Jon. An eclipse passes and the sun re-emerges. Let them be patient with us O God. Behind the moon the sun still shines.

August 11. We returned home from LBI. Re-entry is hard and the days are excruciating emotionally. I went to lunch with my prayer group yesterday which was difficult to do. I went to see our car dealer and dear friend Charlie F. about transferring Jon's car to Brad, Jon's closest friend. Aunt Fran came for dinner last night. Paige called sobbing for her Uncle Jon. We received a gift of a little book, Lament for a Son, written by Nicholas Wolterstorff, another pastor and bereaved father. It helped some. But his son died in a tragic climbing accident; mine died because of the pernicious evil of addiction. I think I should write my own such book. Maybe that's what this is.

We've moved officially out of the numb stage of grief; now it is brutally raw. I sleep okay, but awaken to the final image of Jon, dead in his room, lips blue, blood and mucous in nose and mouth, still not cold, but life gone. So I get up, grieve through my shower, which is my tear closet. I follow the disciplines of my morning routine, go for a walk. Jean has slept in lately, so I don't wait, but go alone, before the heat. Grief is isolating. Grief is done alone. If not careful, grief can separate you for ever. Watch your step!

I sat awhile in Jon's room last night until the sadness drove me out. Jon's death has left a hole in our future. Julia feels it too. She relied upon him for so much. We might have too, in the future when we are old, and if he had straightened out. We both supposed that Jon would ultimately be the one to lean on should we advance in years. There is aloneness in the world. "Alone" is the first "not good" in the Bible: it is not good that the man should be alone. When the future is stolen, you stop making plans and dreaming dreams about it. Of course, this is not the whole future. We are in an eclipse. We now have a different future up ahead, one of which we have not had time to dream or imagine.

Our soon to arrive granddaughter Caitlyn is breech and scheduled to arrive by C-section next Wednesday, Mark and Michele's second child. One life gone, a new one arrives. Generations come, generations go, says the preacher. All is vanity and a striving after wind. By the way, what is the balance between tragedy and mercy, between a great demonic evil and a providential snatching away and taking home? Who knows what Jon might have become? Who knows what he and we have been spared? And, surely, our meaning and purpose are not extinguished by leaving here, just as they don't begin here but have their genesis in the mind of God. But "here" is what we know best, though not well at all. Who really fully understands the mystery of life and the wonders of creation? All of our science and our reason are but child's play still.

Saturday night: our grandson Logan's second birthday party is at Julia's apartment. Jon's friends and ex-girlfriends all gather there. It's okay. We continue to take incoming hits of intense grief. I plan to return to the pulpit a week from tomorrow. We battle for each ounce of comfort and understanding. Reason is battered into silence before the mysteries of life, suffering and death. I'm beginning to brush up against the edges of just a few who seem surprised that we're not improving, not "getting over it". They just don't understand. Those who love most will hurt the longest.

Chapter XIV

Navigating the River of Tears

Almost one month after Jon died our granddaughter Caitlyn was born by caesarian section. Jean was asked to come to Plumville in western Pennsylvania where Mark and Michele live, to care for our grandson Jackson while Mark went to the hospital in Kittanning for the birth and follow up care and support. I thought it would be good for Jean to go to get her away from home if only for a short while. It was difficult for her but Jean's answer to their request was never in doubt. They needed her and she would be there. Still, she had to fight off the paralysis of her grief and her apprehension over the long ride by herself, to make the trip.

I missed her but also welcomed the brief stint of simply dealing with my own grief on my own schedule and my own terms in solitude. While she was gone I cleaned the house from top to bottom to try to make her homecoming a pleasant surprise. A clean house does little to comfort a mother's broken heart. Nothing really seems to bring healing. All the little things I've done over the years as ways to say, "I love you," seem so small and useless compared with the sorrow that is as deep in Jean as any canyon under the Pacific Ocean. Still I continue to do them and I know she does appreciate them; they just cannot help what needs helping.

Caitlyn came into the world on August 18th. She was healthy and beautiful and added to the blessing of our growing family. When all were safely home and settled, Jean returned and the beat went on.

Journal entry, August 28th: five weeks in:

The grief has been difficult and demanding. I'm back in the pulpit and on the job pretty much. I still experience sadness in great waves. I have frequent days that I have named "sad days". When they strike, I leave the office and go home. Thank God I have a job and a congregation that allows for this. How do those with no such luxury navigate through a time such as this?

I'm trying to be a good husband to Jean. Over 80% of couples who lose a child experience the end of their marriage as well. May it never be so with us. I sense a great gulf between us, an ocean of grief over which it is nearly impossible to reach and touch one another in any way that will help at all.

Friday nights are the hardest for me. I wake up at 3 AM each week and rehearse the events and images over and over. Jean does the same. I'm aware of her lying awake beside me, reliving and grieving. She is still isolating herself from others. The interaction with caring people is still too hard. Church folks continue to be kind. We try to walk each day and take at least one outing together. Daily trips to Starbucks for over priced lattes provide cheap therapy. My faith is proving strong, but I have heavy bouts of futility: "Who cares?", and "What does it matter?"

Tuesday after Labor Day, at Mark's. Grieving goes on unabated.

We went to Mark's again for Caitlyn's baptism. Michele's family was there as well and Mark invited me to participate in the liturgy. It was a proud moment for us all save for one thing: the attack of grief that came upon Jean early in the service as the congregation broke into singing the hymn, "How Great Thou Art." The next thing I knew, I saw her being crushed under the weight of sorrow. At the first opportunity she slipped out and walked back to Mark's home to try to recover. I stayed on and finished the service alongside Mark, my son of whom I was so proud.

Unbeknownst to Jean, the party after worship to celebrate the occasion included a number of guests from Mark's congregation. It would not be family only. Before we arrived home, people whom Jean did not know began ringing the doorbell, all cheerful and bringing gifts of food for the gathering and settling in awaiting our arrival. Jean was vulnerable and simply became overwhelmed with her emotions.

When I arrived I found her weeping in an upstairs bedroom. It became obvious that we were not going to be able to socialize as the occasion required. We had to make our apologies, pack up, and head for home. Feelings of hurt and disappointment coursed through the family, and perhaps a measure of incomprehension in some folks. Many were sympathetic and concerned. We were sorry but we were at the mercy of a sorrow that we could not manage. It was stronger than our ability to tame it with politeness or courtesy of any kind. The joy of the day was no match for it. We were reacting in the only way we knew how just to keep from sinking deeper into the mire of our own broken hearts: we ran.

Within minutes, our light luggage was loaded up, we said brief, uncomfortable goodbyes and we were on our way home to New Jersey, a five to six hour drive.

Jean sat inches from me and sobbed for hours on end as I drove onward feeling totally helpless. I knew there was really nothing I could say or do, so we travelled on in silence, alone together. Her tears abated somewhere near Harrisburg after four hours of steady, intense grieving. We both felt remorse for the situation we'd left behind and for the pain we had caused Mark and Michele but felt powerless to do anything other than what we did. We ran for cover, for the haven of our own home, away from the view of anyone. We had to trust that in time we might be understood and forgiven.

Journal entry:

September 16th: Another Friday. My grief is changing ever so slightly. I'm working more but with great effort. Jean and I are talking openly and well. Lately we've been facing the fact that things with Jon were headed into some very bad seasons. Addiction is the disease from hell. It does him no dishonor for us to acknowledge that we are experiencing some relief from the hell he was already putting us through and some relief that that part of our suffering is now over. We'd take him back in a minute and continue the fight if it were possible, which of course it is not.

Jean is experiencing a deep disappointment with God. We don't either of us want to say that, at least not too loudly. Jean was willing to face any challenge save one: the death of her child. She thought she'd be spared. She was not. Nor was I. Can God hear us whisper through our tears? How good is God's hearing? Did God hear our prayers all through those pain-wracked years of Julia's rebellion and Jon's addiction? Will this grief make me tough but not bitter, or just bitter and not tough?

Grieving is full of paradoxical opposites that refuse union. Devastation and relief. Mercy and punishment (the punishment of relentless sorrow). Good and evil. God and the devil. Divine sovereignty and divine permission in the war in heaven and on earth. Surely goodness and mercy shall follow me all the days of my life, but I am also being stalked by a malevolent enemy who seeks to break and destroy me and all whom I love and all that I hold dear.

Friday: the day after tomorrow I must preach again. How flat and uninspired I feel. I'm unable to muster enthusiasm on time. I'm functioning on grit and determination, and I hope, on the power of the Holy Spirit. I don't feel much Holy or much Spirit. Mostly just sadness. I try to fight the depression, give thanks to God for life and blessings still remaining, and move through the daily disciplines of life: shave, shower, brush my teeth and hair, eat, sleep, work, live and keep living even when I wonder what the point of it all might be.

Chapter XV

Bankruptcy

Date unknown:
I must have read a book that counseled me to list my losses.
Here is a partial list:

- *My youngest son.*
- *A wife who can be happy. I've gained a broken hearted mate.*
- *The future with Jon in it, even though it looked as though it would be deeply clouded with drug addiction and who knows what horrors.*
- *Jon's mirth, coolness, sense of humor, and energy.*
- *Jon's love for music.*
- *His presence for Jean when I go away.*
- *His presence for me and all the rest who loved him so dearly. He's gone. He touched many, many people in his too short life.*
- *His times with Austin, his counselor and my friend, are over.*
- *His listening with respect to my sermon tapes and his appreciation.*
- *His love and admiration for me as his dad.*
- *Our heart to heart talks.*
- *The opportunity to fight for his life.*
- *Times when I could teach him things.*

- *Times when he'd ask my advice or seek my approval.*
- *Adventures we should have had.*
- *His support when I grow old.*

Some things which remain, some in different form:
- *His love for us.*
- *My love for him.*
- *Memories. Photographs*
- *Constant evolving sorrow.*

September 21st: I had the first inklings of life that can flow out of the death.

Chapter XVI

Life in the Rearview Mirror

For most of my thirty years in ministry, I have been a member of a small prayer group, mostly comprised of fellow clergy men. The members have come and gone, but I've always had four to six other men to meet with weekly for encouragement and support, men who know how to listen without trying to fix, men who only give advice when asked for, men who will accept me for who I am and who are faithfully present in my life over the long haul.

I remember sharing in my group, probably early in the fall of the year that Jon died, how I felt like I was living in others' rearview mirror. The lives of people all around me were continuing on down the highway, but I was still standing by the side of the grief road watching them being absorbed into whatever future life awaited them. They could see me standing like a forlorn hitchhiker who had no hope of catching a ride, my reflection in the mirror growing smaller and smaller as the distance between us steadily widened. I didn't begrudge them getting on with their own lives. I never expected them to stay with me too long in a grief that only those in it can really understand. And I wouldn't wish this terrible knowledge on an enemy, let alone a friend, this knowing what it's like to lose a child.

Still it was a lonely insight. Like all the raw insights this loss has provided me, it helped to articulate it and have others hear it, but not much. Still, I found myself wondering how others would face such gut wrenching enlightenment with none to listen and affirm the insight.

I have always been grateful for the existence of this group of men with whom to be vulnerable and real, a "band of brothers", but never so much as now. I felt apologetic for subjecting them to my week in and week out rehearsals of the progress and the pain of my journey of grief, but they never begrudged me their attention and their care.

I've had a longstanding compassion upon the men of our culture who try to journey as lone rangers in the masculine enterprise and end up as empty posers, putting forth some caricature of what they think a man is while lacking the genuine spiritual vitality of Jesus of Nazareth, who was so convicting in his authenticity that humans finally tried to get rid of him by hanging him on the cross. But now, I really couldn't fathom how any man would attempt to walk this lonely walk without at least having some deep and lasting relationships with other men as brothers at least within earshot.

Very soon, I found myself searching for some sort of honest answer to the question, "How are you doing?" After one thousand utterances of "I'm hanging in there," I found I just didn't want to say it anymore, but I did appreciate people asking. And not everyone did ask. Some were mute because they feared that to ask was to increase my pain, as though bringing it up would remind me of a pain that I'd managed to forget. No such forgetting was possible. Some were silent because they simply did not know what to say or perhaps they feared they would say the wrong thing, which is of course a distinct possibility. Mercifully, no one said "It must have been God's will," or, "God works all things together for good," or some of the other clichés which are threadbare from overuse, not to mention being cruel when used in the wrong situation.

Once in a while, someone would flirt with doing damage with their mouth, but I was in fact surprised at how respectful most people were. And I became increasingly adept at gently correcting people if I sensed they were heading in a bad direction.

This flirts with the hurting one needing to instruct the caregivers, but it was really a form of self defense, and besides, sometimes the caregivers do need instruction.

One of the most discouraging experiences which happened numerous times occurred when someone would ask how I was doing and I began to actually tell them, thinking they wanted to know, and then to have them change the subject and begin to tell me of someone they knew that was going through a hard time or had experienced a loss. I rediscovered what I already knew, that good listeners are a rare treasure.

So I searched for a brief answer that would be a door opener for someone who really wanted to know how I was faring, but one that did not make listening mandatory for someone who was just saying "Hi" with the question, "How are you doing?"

Some possibilities:

"I'm hurting like hell!" (This did not seem too useful for pastor/parishioner communication, but was fairly accurate.)

"Not bad for the shape I'm in" (Too trite).

"I've joined a club nobody wants to join." (Not bad.)

"I'm learning a lot." (Too arcane.)

"One day at a time." (Threadbare)

"I'm okay. I'm fine." (All lies, but most simple)

I made other feeble attempts to gain a handle on negotiating the social landscape which is contorted beyond recognition by this grief, but I simply can't remember ever solving the dilemma I faced in this regard. Soon enough the intensity of peoples' inquiries subsided and I receded into superficial responses which would let both of us get on with our day. The pain was increasingly privatized.

Chapter XVII

Trips

W hat began with the gift of our stay on Long Beach Island became a steady stream of the restorative love of God in my life. I did not know the scope that this would assume at the time. It was a successive unfolding of journeys provided by the Lord through God's people that became an important element in my own healing process.

Dear friends Barbara and Ron Barrett in San Diego phoned. "We have accumulated frequent flier miles and we were praying and believe God has directed us to give them to you so that you can come for a visit to California." Jean had never been there and had wanted to go for some time. We accepted.

We were emotionally flat-lining still in late October when we went. We spent a day at the San Diego Zoo. We ate fish tacos down on the waterfront. We saw beautiful beaches, seals in the cove at La Jolla, took a day long driving loop, sun roof open, just the two of us in our friends' Volvo, freely and generously offered, out into the desert, north into apple and pineapple country, around and down through Torre Pines State Park with its majestic Pacific vistas overlooking miles of white sandy beaches. Surfers everywhere were painful reminders of Jon. The beauty that should have provided an escape, however momentary, mixed with sorrow as it was, served instead as a painful signal that we had only just begun our long trek through the emotional desert. You can run, you can fly 3,000 miles from home, but you can't hide! Still, in all, I felt gratitude for the love of God flowing through the generosity of our friends. We ate, we shared fellowship, we saw much beauty, we worshipped in their church, we flew back home. We continued our hard grieving. Many more excursions would come our way in the coming months.

Chapter XVIII

Fellowship of the Broken- hearted

I had a parishioner who came to see me in January, the year after Jon died. Her forty-three year old son had died that December just a few days before Christmas and I had no clue. I told her as we sat in my study that I'd had no idea that she had lost him, and she said she just couldn't tell me before, fearing that it would hurt me too much. During the next hour or so, we sat and shared our pain. It was a profound experience of the fellowship of suffering.

Far from being hurtful, it was a great comfort. Just for a few moments, the isolation of grief was broken. I glimpsed how sorrow could be converted into comfort. It was one of the early experiences of mining the gold that is embedded in the sorrow. There have been many more since. I knew how to be in the room with her, how to be in that conversation, confident that I would not say the wrong thing, that I would not abuse nor misuse her sorrow. In those moments, I was the best pastor I'd ever been.

Now, nearly four years later, this same woman just lost her husband. He went to the hospital for heart surgery, which he survived, but they could never stabilize him. I conducted the funeral, yesterday at this writing. The connection between our hearts has continued and I could feel both her gratitude and her trust as I spoke the words of comfort inherent in our faith and as I commended her husband to the mercy of God and her and her family to God's consolations. But underneath the courageous exterior that the numbness that newborn grief causes and allows, she is headed into another season of raw emotions, the time of another devastating absence, of holes not easily filled, of tears not readily dried, and of a broken heart not quickly to be mended.

One of the painful insights in the aftermath of Jon's death was the realization of how miserably I had failed parishioners in the past when they lost their children. I did pretty well at the time of death and through the funeral, but did very poorly with follow up care. I was like so many that I have experienced since losing Jon. They were caught in *my* rearview mirror. I asked several for forgiveness when I had the opportunity. I had been as clueless as many who surround me even now.

All whom I approached were kind and gracious and seemed to release me from any debt I owed them. I am so grateful for their gift of mercy toward me. In turn, I try to be as merciful to those who miss me in my hour of need as well. And I have resolved to be a better pastor in the future, but I know I will make many more mistakes, miss many an opportunity to bring comfort, and continue to live in my very imperfect skin.

Journal entry: February 10, 2006, half way into the seventh month.

Months have passed since my last journal entry. The grief tsunami hit again after New Year's Day, especially on Jean. She's in a really intense period now, having bad dreams and much anger. We soldier on. In prayer the other day, Larry, who is a member of my prayer group, asked Jesus to come alongside, first Jean, and then me. As he prayed, I received a mental picture of walking with Jesus between Jean and myself. He had one arm around each of us and said simply, "I am with you, and Jon is with me." This was profoundly comforting.

Soon after, I had lunch with a colleague who gave me a copy of an out of print book by John Claypool, The Tracks of a Fellow Struggler, which included the text of four sermons he preached in the aftermath of the death of his one year old daughter who died of leukemia. This was very good and helpful to us both.

I've begun the process of applying for a sabbatical grant from the Lilly Endowment, which would provide money and four months time away. I can only dream and imagine what a blessing this would be for both Jean and me.

T. D. Jakes said in a sermon lately which I saw on TV something to the effect that when we meet our pain we run to our sin. I think it was Frederick Buechner who wrote that our sin is our carefully constructed defense against the presence of God, which is profoundly true. But it is also often our lame attempt to anesthetize ourselves against the pain and sometimes the ennui of daily life as well. My soul craves healing, but will settle for anesthesia. With this grief, there is no effective anesthesia, neither through faith nor through sin.

Chapter XVIX

A Little Theological Reflection on Sin and Other Solutions

"Sorrow is like an arrow in the breast-the more vigorously the deer runs in order to run away from it, the more firmly the arrow becomes embedded in it."

Soren Kierkegaard [1]

"Oh Lord, not only do you know our sorrow better than do we ourselves, but you feel it, too. You understand the burden, the heavy grief that we bear. Make us humble, therefore, so that in our rebellion against life's injustices we do not turn for comfort to those who are like wandering stars, or to those who are like the raging waves of the sea foaming out their own shame. You are our refuge and our strength, and there is none other."

Soren Kierkegaard [2]

When we meet our pain we run to our sin. I can remember the place and the day that I stopped believing in sin. I was sitting in the school auditorium for what they called assembly. I was thirteen years old, in seventh grade. Mr. G., teacher of economics was onstage but I don't have the faintest recollection of what he was talking about. I remember he exuded Ivy League sophistication. As he strutted in his intellectual pride, he made some sideways comment about sin with a sneer of ridicule in his manner and tone, the implication being that only shallow, naive rubes would believe such nonsense in our modern age.

And that was all she wrote. I figured that the idea of sin was simply a tool adults used for social control and to prevent people like me from satisfying their hungers and having loads of fun in the process. I was out the internal doorway and into the wide world of license and self-gratification. It would be a few years before the change inside would be manifested in visible behaviors. I first had to gain more freedom from parental controls. I really had no idea of the damage I was about to inflict upon myself and many others.

The outward behaviors we call sins are really just the manifestation of what in Christian theology is called the sin nature which constitutes the underlying matrix out of which the specific and varied behaviors called sins arise. It is with this flaw that we all enter the world. Modern secular thinkers would dispute this but I think the preponderance of evidence in favor of this view is overwhelming here. After all, how many perfect people do you know?

We look at a little baby and see innocence. No wrongs have been committed, nor could they be by such a cherubic little angel. But the baby grows. What once was rightly used to signal the need for care, crying, soon becomes a tool to manipulate and control the world. What develops as a necessary psychological structure for organizing the world into a coherent existence, the ego, soon becomes a little potentate who loves to play god.   The sin nature leads us into many a blind alley and into frustrating dead ends. It excuses us when we take advantage of others for our own benefit. The sin nature gives rise to the destructive behaviors we call sins. The Bible rightly sums up the predictable outcome: "The wages of sin is death"

The Christian answer to this dilemma is summed up by the Apostle Paul when he says: "I have been crucified with Christ, and it is no longer I who live, but it is Christ who lives in me; and the life I now live in the flesh I live by faith in the Son of God who loved me and gave himself for me." (Galatians 2:20) The old nature needs to be replaced; it must be put in its place. There needs to be a revolution in the soul which results in a change of government. I must acknowledge that I am not master of my fate nor am I captain of my soul. The ego needs to be dethroned and take its rightful place at the feet of Jesus.

Self centered existence is put to death; Christ centered existence replaces it. The former results in selfishness, in all sorts of brokenness and futility, in betrayals, and finally in death from which there is no escape. The latter cleanses and heals our character and transforms death from a dead end to an entry way into a brand new mode of being. Dying with Christ by faith here leads to abundant life here. Dying in Christ at the end of our life here opens upon life eternal.

Therefore we do not grieve as those who have no hope. Death claims to be the ultimate end of all things individual. "You may live a short life or a long life, but in the end, I, death, am all you get." The resurrection of Jesus Christ exposes the pretense of this arrogant imposter we know as death. Our grief is invaded by hope.

Whenever I hear the words of Jesus warning those who would cause a little one to stumble, I wonder about Mr. G. I don't blame him, but stumble I did. He provided the occasion for me to trip, but I embarked upon the whole series of choices that would prove to be so expensive. I was ripe for the picking and had he not come along, someone else would have. It is a sobering thought to think how even off-handed comments may lead someone young and impressionable astray.

If the sin nature is truly dead through faith in Christ, to what do we run when we experience so devastating a loss as the loss of a child? Sometimes it will be to old familiar sinful behaviors, the ones we tried before knowing Christ in our attempt to anesthetize our selves against the pain of our inner aloneness or to distract us from our anxieties and our despair. So we may circle back and seek comfort through old solutions to our inner void. But there will be no meaningful comfort found here.

Indulging in sin is like taking a drink is to a recovering alcoholic; the problem is not the one drink, but the addiction which is fueled by the drink. The one drink promises to satisfy the longing but leads only to greater and greater thirst. The sin nature knows what feeds it and craves the food that will sustain it. If the sin nature were a personified character, we might see it lurking outside the graveyard hoping for a resurrection of its own. Even if individual sins or ineffective solutions to our sorrow are taken up, there will be no resurrection for the sin nature once crucified with Christ. And sinful attempts to mollify our sorrow are doomed to leave us more empty than we were before.

There are sins, and there are seemingly less noxious attempts involving false solutions that do not yield the results our souls really need. So we might immerse ourselves in comfort food, or in sex, or drugs, or alcohol, or pornography, or escapist fantasies, or work, or adultery, or pride, or adventure, or travel. Some are sins. Some are merely mistakes. The list could be expanded but the point is clear. These are a few of the most obvious choices, though not all solutions to our pain are sinful in themselves. Whether by sins or by ineffective solutions we try to comfort ourselves in our sorrow, we will fail to be comforted when we try to gain from them what we should be receiving from Christ.

Sex for example is for procreation, pleasure, and intimacy. It is not properly used as a form of anesthesia. Work is good unless it becomes a compulsive place to hide from our relationships or our heart condition. It is God's gift that we take pleasure in all our toil. It is misguided when we lose our sense of vocation in our work and return to cultivating the cursed ground of compulsion which neither relies on God nor honors nor trusts in God's good provision. It is a denial of our redemption when we labor like Adam among the thistles and thorns and feel that what we need is supplied grudgingly by both nature and God. Eating is a great pleasure. We eat to live; it is a mistake when we live to eat. Grief can cause things like sex and food and work, and many other basic things of life to become idolatrous and twisted.

Less obvious temptations are the inner vows not to take risks anymore, not to be vulnerable or expose ourselves to further hurts. We begin to close up. Inner fortresses are a natural response to being wounded and may serve us well for a time. The problem is that they tend to endure long past the season where they serve a useful function. What once served to protect us then becomes a prison cell of emotional and spiritual confinement.

As we live with the Holy Spirit and inner healing increases inner freedom, we grow open and vulnerable once again and develop a healthy balance of wisdom and courage for living. When such a severe wound is sustained as happens in child loss or other tragedies, the temptation is to reconstruct fortresses around our own hearts, perhaps undoing, for a time at least, years of work done in getting free and emerging into the light of Christ.

The problem is that these sins and defenses and idols were and still are dead things that lead nowhere. They are dead ends. There is no life to be found here. They were dead when we first exchanged them for new life in Christ. They are still dead. They waste our time and deliver us no real comfort. They deepen our distress and our isolation and sooner or later will have to be forsaken all over again. We must run to Christ, not to our sin. He is our high tower and our strong defense. We find real comfort in the Lord, not in the cold dungeons we have constructed out of the bricks of our sorrow.

Chapter XX

Running to Jesus

O ne way we have learned to run to Christ is in worship. Worship opens us up and connects us to deep levels of vulnerability. Worship in Spirit and in truth not only pleases the Lord but also holds up a mirror so that we behold the state of our inner being. That's why so many have their most troubling thoughts sitting in worship on a Sunday morning. Real worship creates an encounter with what is really present between the living God and the living person.

But what if one has been busy at work constructing a safe place to hide from either sins or sorrows? Or what if one has found ways to build inner defenses against the raw emotions of grief only to have the powerful tenderness of the Lord dismantle them in the encounter with the Holy Spirit that is central in true worship. I have seen more than one bereaved person leave in the middle of a service in an uncontrollable flood of emotions and tears, the most difficult to see being my own wife, my beloved Jean, and that more than once after Jon died. In fact Jean chose not to attend worship or other church functions for some time after our loss because it was not emotionally safe for her to do so. She did not want her raw emotions to be on public display and she never knew what might trigger a powerful wave of grief that would completely swamp her.

I recall one widow in my first pastorate who began attending shortly after she lost her husband. She wore very dark wrap-around sunglasses to worship for nearly a year. She would slip in late and slip out early. Eventually the glasses came off and her joy in living returned, but it was a risky and slow process for her, and I admired her courage and determination. Just recently, a widower whose wife had died a year before greeted me at the door and said that it was in church, in worship, where he missed his wife the most.

If the heart is flooded with sorrow, then sorrow will be drawn up and out in worship. If the heart is filled with guilt, worship will induce conviction with a view to repentance and forgiveness. If the heart is filled with shame, worship will become a pathway to acceptance and consolation as the Holy Spirit covers and heals the wounds at the core of that condition. Every heart condition has a commensurate working of the Holy Spirit offered in the encounter called worship.

How hard it has been to be the pastor in these moments when my wife would suddenly slip out the side door, to be the man up front who must stay at his post and keep things moving along, putting off my urge to care for her until later when I got home. Perhaps if I were there beside her I could gently take her hand or place my arm around her shoulder, reaching out in some small way. As it was though, I was left to wonder what hit my wife and why and how. Was it a hymn I chose, or was it something I said, or was it something that I had nothing to do with? I would usually find out eventually. Maybe I would be able to comfort her, but often I was not. The sorrow was simply beyond my ability to fix.

Sometimes it would be me who'd get clobbered by grief, right in the middle of my own sermon. Many years ago I read a book by Harry Emerson Fosdick about preaching. He said something that caught my attention and has stayed with me for many years. It was that preaching is the central act of worship for the preacher. In preaching it is true that there I am most open and most vulnerable. It is in preaching that I feel most present to God and most dependent upon the Holy Spirit. Those minutes in the pulpit are most vibrant and alive with the sense of God's presence. On many an occasion since Jon's death, I have experienced a sharp stabbing pain while preaching and had to continue on through a powerful wave of emotions.

Or what are we to make of prayer? If our big prayers, like "Lord, please spare my child's life," receive no answer or the answer, "No," then why bother? Prayer is the most available and most intimate of all relational connections with our Savior. Deep disappointments or gashing wounds like child loss can make prayer seem pointless, a useless activity to be consigned to the ash heap of unbelief. When a child dies we are forced to confront the questions that arise out of the sense of the pointlessness of prayer.

The only avenue open to us here is to be brazenly, brutally honest in our conversation with the Lord. Anything short of this we will know for certain to be a sham. In child loss the bland middle ground of passionless prayers is forcibly removed by intense sorrow. Honest prayer takes courage, boldness, and trust that our relationship is strong enough to endure the harsh interactions of anguish.

Fortunately for me, I had been schooling myself in praying the Psalms for many years and had already come to know and appreciate the permission given by the Holy Spirit in giving us these inspired prayers to be fearlessly honest. An attentive reading of the Psalms, or better yet, a practice of praying them, put me in touch with the wide range of human emotions permitted, even encouraged by God in prayer. God not only allows, but God expects us to be genuine when we would speak with God.

Most of us begin praying with so many religious preconceptions that our prayers are far too timid. We don't think it is appropriate to tell God what we really think or feel, so we end up saying words we think God will be pleased to hear. In other words, we lie. In the anguish of losing a child, we know that lies will not help us in the least. The communion we seek has to be real or it is nothing at all.

Chapter XXI

Questions and Trust

To run to him, we must trust him, and this is the rub. The death of a child throws a spear into our capacity to trust. If my child can die, anything can happen. The world can come to seem like a vicious, frightening place. Most of our trust involves some notion of being protected, which in reality is not the central promise given by God, even though I am convinced that no one knows the massive levels of protection we actually do receive in the course of a normal day.

How many personal incidents of divine protection we have each received is impossible to know. It is a mercy that we have no idea of all the things that could have happened to us that were prevented. Were we given to see the level of threat constantly near us, living would be an exercise in terror. So we live life blind and insensible, taking far too much for granted. This presumption easily develops into an unjustified sense of entitlement. We come to assume that we are entitled to escape suffering and sorrow. This is simply not true. The degree to which we do escape calamities and sorrows is a gratuitous operation of sheer grace.

What is promised overtly by Jesus is His presence: I will be with you. I will never leave you nor forsake you. My grace is sufficient for you. In the world you will have tribulation, but be of good cheer, I have overcome the world. Lo, I am with you always to the close of the age. And so on and on the words of scripture pour out, cascading in our direction.

Yes, but is presence enough? No one wants to hurt this badly. Jesus prayed, "If it be possible let this cup pass from me." This prayer we can pray without hesitation. But we stop short of the "nevertheless" of Jesus in Gethsemane: nevertheless, not what I will but what you will. For us who have lost a child the brutally inexplicable answer to the cry to be spared was, "no". The cup did not pass by. We've been forced to drink it down to the dregs.

But unlike Jesus and his Father, it is difficult if not impossible for us to see the death of our child as being wrapped up in some greater redemptive purpose. We now know that the death of Jesus was to effect the salvation of the world's lost people. The death of our child seems inexplicable and pointless, a waste of life and love and human potential. What are we to do with this? How can we ever make sense of it? Was this death God's will? Did God who is good and all powerful cause it, or simply allow it? And if God allowed it, why on earth did God allow it?

I have known for many years that the questions involving the goodness of God and the presence of evil, what the theologians call the questions of theodicy, are unanswerable. The issues of God's self limitation as God limits his own sovereignty and steps back far enough to allow us room the make free choices for good or ill are great mysteries. What is the relationship between freedom and love? Can there be genuine love in the absence of freedom. To say a meaningful "yes", I must have an authentic opportunity to say "no". The risks God takes daily to allow lost people the freedom to make deadly choices because freedom is tightly tied to the prospect of love becoming real, are issues that finally lead us all to the frontier of our capacity to give a logical explanation of the nature of things. Our minds strain to know the answers to our unanswerable questions surrounding the goodness of God and the prevalence of evil. I suspect the answers are concealed and will ultimately be revealed by an unpacking of the theological and biblical assertion that God is love.

In the grief involved in losing a child, most questions lead nowhere but increased emotional and spiritual torment. How can we ever trust again in the goodness and kindness of the one who promises to be with us when we feel so forsaken and so alone?

These and all similar questions are frightening for us to entertain. The problem is that they are well nigh impossible to ignore. They are no longer academic exercises involving hypothetical life situations. Now the issues are excruciatingly real. It takes dogged persistence to keep putting ourselves, questions and all, in the paths of grace. My own belief is that this persistence, even this, is no work of my own. It too arrives from the hand of the God that refuses to let me go, no matter what. It is God's relentlessly loving hand that saves us from perdition.

Descartes has been credited with the adage, "I think, therefore I am." Western enlightenment culture took the saying and ran with it, thus spawning a radical reductionism of what it means to be human. We came to think that only that which is rational is valuable or true. We lost sight of other crucial factors that contribute to our being human, central of which is the capacity and the need to give and receive love.

Along with this, what about our use of sign and symbol, of myth and metaphor, our imaginative ability to create worlds within and to alter the world without in accordance with our inner vision, and so on and on. Our intellect has become proud and demanding. In times of grief, it demands to be satisfied, insisting that if all our questions were answered, then we could be healed and go on with living in a rational world with no ambiguity and no enduring agony. This is simply false in my view. It excludes far too much.

I am reminded of a call I received very soon after I graduated from seminary and entered the pastoral ministry. A young couple who had a very slim connection with my congregation, having attended a few times quite a few years in the past, had just lost their two year old son. I was summoned to the house to bring pastoral care and comfort and handle the subsequent funeral. I remember feeling like a total green horn, in way over my head, which is not unusual for me even today. Seminary did not prepare me for this. I doubt that there is any preparation to be gained in a classroom for times such as these in any event.

I anticipated being bombarded with questions that I knew I could not answer. So I prayed, and I received an answer in my mind that I believe was counsel from the Holy Spirit. It was, "Even if you could answer their questions, they will still have a broken heart. Your job is to go and be present." It was a liberating insight to discover that I was not called to be a religious answer man. I was simply to go and be the presence of the loving Christ in this horrible sorrow. As young and untested as I was at that point, somehow I still believe I got it right.

Journal entry: March 3rd, 2006. The photo collages assembled by Julia and Jon's friends for display at the funeral still stand in one corner of our living room. Jon looks out at us all, at me, from the snapshots of a short lifetime. He is present, but painfully absent. If I'm the head of the family, I sit atop a seething caldron of sorrow, anguish of heart and soul, anger, and disappointment, none of which can I fix or even ameliorate in any way. And I have my own struggles, sins, relapses, pangs, arrows which are more like spears which randomly pierce me just for the hell of it.

Our dear friends John and Linda will arrive for a visit this afternoon, coming down from New Hampshire. I'm eager to see them and to have them here. This is a lonely place. I feel the urge to never leave nor forsake the grieving place. I need at least a handful of people to remember and share, who will listen patiently, not change the subject, and not go away.

A couple from the church has agreed to take Jon's mattress and box spring. This is a major step forward. I am starting to get anxious to change his basement room back to a study for me, which it was before he returned home the last time. Everything is hard as hell! His clothes still hang in several closets. Many of the artifacts of Jon's life sit in the same spot as the night he died. The time will come which is not yet to take these relics of his life to some other spot.

Journal entry: March 25th, 2006. "And a sword will pierce your heart also." How hard was it for Mary to see old Simeon's prophecy come true through the death of her beloved son? How hard for Jesus to press into an obedience that he knew would be that piercing sword, but which he also knew would be the source of hers and everyone else's salvation? What a poignant piercing he too endured, as hanging on the cross he watched first hand as his own mother's heart was pierced by the grief sword. Still, he ministers: woman behold your son, an agonizing double entendre. Does he mean, turn your eyes to John? He will be your replacement son. Or does he mean, "Look full face upon me. Look what has become of me. Let this gruesome visage divest you of all your alternative plans for me, and see me as I am." Woman, behold your son. In this brutalized vision of your child, you will see, if you dare to look closely enough, the Savior of the world. Surely this was an impenetrable mystery for a mother.

Chapter XXII

Combat

You may think me a medievalist, a throwback to the dark ages, when I tell you that I think we have a real, cosmic enemy who operates with real intelligence and plots malevolent stratagems to hurt us, to steal God's good gifts from us, and yes, to kill us if he can. This admission may cause you to hold me in contempt, to which I simply say that Jesus gave credence to his existence, encountering Satan at each step along the path of his ministry. There was the battle for his heart after his baptism and forty days of fasting in the wilderness. Every time I study these texts and set out to preach upon them, I am astounded by the subtlety and multi-layered complexity of these clever enticements for Jesus to sin. I am also in awe of Jesus simple and powerful rebuttals of the attempts made to steal his heart away from his Father.

Satan tried again as he co-opted the mind and imagination and the friendship of Peter, using Peter's voice to try to dissuade Jesus from going to Jerusalem and a certain execution. How Peter must have been stung by Jesus rebuke, "Get behind me Satan. You are not on the side of God but on the side of men." I doubt that Satan anticipated the Cross as the ultimate weapon of God's victory. He saw it rather as his ultimate weapon making death as agonizingly brutal as he could incite the minds of men to conceive.

The great Apostle Paul acknowledged the reality of our enemy when he said, "Finally, be strong in the Lord and in the strength of his power. Put on the whole armor of God so that you may be able to stand against the wiles of the devil. For our struggle is not against enemies of blood and flesh, but against the rulers, against the authorities, against the cosmic powers of this present darkness, against the spiritual forces of evil in the heavenly places." Ephesians 6:10-12

And again the writer of Hebrews says, "Since therefore, the children share flesh and blood, he himself likewise shared the same things, so that through death he might destroy the one who has the power of death, that is, the devil, and free those who all their lives were held in slavery by the fear of death." Hebrews 2:14-15. A quick glance in a concordance will point to many other Bible texts that place one like me in good company. But then not everyone who loses a child believes the Bible. I do.

Fifteen years ago, I dealt with this problem involving world views extensively as I wrote my doctoral dissertation and I have no desire to duplicate that work now. I will only say here that I think western intellectual culture made a serious blunder in becoming rationalistic to the exclusion of supernatural dimensions of experience. I simply find that I can make no sense of the conditions in this life which can be so painful to endure without an acknowledgment of a transpersonal, trans-generational malevolent adversary who is very good at what he does.

Too many wounds sustained by so many seem surgically administered, often in early childhood through the agency of abusive adults and the seductive doctrines of demons at large in the world. But this is only part of the story. The real situation involves the interplay of the unholy trinity of the world, the flesh, and the devil. Our world is contorted by thousands of years of human sin, our humanity is gnarled by countless choices to rebel against God, and we are stalked by demonic evil.

That being said, how shall we live confidently, refusing to be obsessed by the presence of demonic evil and confident in the sovereignty of a loving God, especially in the aftermath of losing a child? Something I came across in the third volume of

Karl Barth's, <u>Church Dogmatics,</u> has proved to be most helpful. He maintained that evil is no thing. It exists only as the negation of that which has positive existence, and therefore we should not stare at it head on but be aware of it with our peripheral vision, all the while maintaining our focus upon Christ. To give examples, think of how darkness disappears the moment the light is switched on, or how hate disappears the moment love enters in, and how guilt is rendered impotent the moment forgiveness is offered and received.

Christ is called "the Lord of glory" by James, Jesus' once unbelieving brother who became a devout believer and the head of the Jerusalem church after Jesus' resurrection. James' faith was so deep that he was martyred in 62 AD, going to death for a belief that he once found impossible to embrace. The word glory is an untranslatable word which carries many nuances of meaning, one of which is weight, another substance. Perhaps another is significance. Christ is the real deal. We focus upon him because he embodies ultimate reality and perfect humanity as well as divinity. Jesus is exactly what God looks like when God becomes human. Jesus' humanity is exactly what we will look like when we are completely redeemed, when we see him face to face and are made perfect like him.

We use the phrase, "I'm only human," to excuse our sins. In actuality, we sin because we have lost the fullness of our created glory and are no longer only human, but have become a mixture of true humanity and humanity distorted by our fallen condition. Just as Jon was living in a bipolar reality, one straight and one stoned, with the two at odds in one body, so are we all a torturous amalgam of holy and fallen. Fortunately for us, God has a vision of us beyond this warring competition and possesses more than enough power to deliver us from this "body of death" as Paul put it at the end of Romans 7.

To bring this back down to earth, I believe that my dear son Jonathan was somehow targeted by Satan. He grew up in a sin saturated environment, with an imperfect father and mother, in a culture of affluence and the easy availability of deadly narcotics, he made his own foolish and ultimately deadly choices, and he was encouraged along the way from malevolent forces from the pit of hell for whom his destruction was a longed for goal. What my faith asserts is that however this demonic purpose was carried out, Jon is not now nor was he ever a trophy of Satan's destructive hatred of all things dear to God, but that Jon is even now a trophy of God's grace.

One may wonder why such venom is directed toward human beings who seem like insignificant targets to draw such intense malevolent fire. I believe the intensity of hatred leveled against us to be commensurate with the passionate love with which God loves us. Satan's real beef is and always has been with God. Once Lucifer, the most beautiful of all the angels, it was his ministry to lead all the praises of heaven. We have no clue why, it is a great mystery, but pride entered into the heart of this great being and he began to covet the glory of God and desire it for himself. Warfare broke out in heaven and one third of the angels were cast out and down to earth. You may argue that this is mythological language and imagery, to which I reply that it is also biblical language. Truth is being conveyed to us from God here.

The surest most effective way to break the heart of a parent is to wound, bruise, and even destroy the child. The central act of demonic hatred was to stir people to crucify the only begotten Son of God. When even the violence and hatred and death on the cross were shown to serve the saving purpose of God's heart, the only thing left was to make war upon the rest of God's children who are in God's family by adoption, included in God's family by a love that has selected us as God's chosen ones. We are both the objects of God's delight, and consequently the objects of the devil's contempt. We focus upon the glory of God in Jesus Christ; we wisely remain aware and vigilant of the presence of malevolent evil which desires our destruction, if for no other reason than just for spite.

Chapter XXIII

A Prophetic Journey:
Thirteen months AD
(After death)

My dear friend Randy had asked me to perform his marriage service on the North Rim of the Grand Canyon. He would pay for Jean and my expenses if I would consent to the honor. I *was* honored and I accepted. We flew into Las Vegas and stayed in the Golden Nugget Hotel and Casino. We partook of a brief draught of the neon reality before heading out to tour Zion National Park, Bryce Canyon, and finally The Grand Canyon.

The scenery was breath-taking and awe inspiring in all three places, each in its own distinctive way. Next to this natural splendor, the artificial glamour of Las Vegas seemed empty. I loved Zion because we viewed it from the floor, looking up at majestic walls of rock. Bryce Canyon was distinctive for the layers of red and the sharp fingers of stone left pointing skyward called hoodoos. And the Grand Canyon is, well, simply grand!

Driving on a day dominated by frequent thunder and lightning and heavy downpours of rain, we found just the right spot for a marriage ceremony on the North rim of the Grand Canyon. We resolved to return the following day. The day was sunny and cool. I conducted the ceremony on a narrow ridge of rock with God's majestic carving of the earth as a backdrop. Randy and Donna's love and friendship as well as the honor it was for me to be asked to lead them in this important moment in their lives was another instance of the amazing love of God being enfleshed and made tangibly real through people who love God and who love us too. Had we had ears able to hear what God was up to at the time, we might have heard the tapping of a celestial hammer on a chisel, chipping away at the great stone of our sorrow. That ability to hear would come later.

One night, in a rustic cabin near the North rim of the canyon, my frequent visitor, insomnia, showed up again. I arose and looked out the door to see, arched above the wide alpine meadow that lay at our door, a stupendous array of God's cosmic artistry in the dazzling display of the stars, undimmed by the competing of city lights endemic to the East coast. I've seen such displays before, in Arkansas, in Maine, on camping trips at various sites east of the Rockies, but the show is never unimpressive. The creative magnificence of our God is truly humbling and astounding. Where were you Job, when I spun the constellations of the heavens across the night sky, just because I wanted to and just because I could? Still, could not he who spun the constellations, could not he who opened the eyes of the blind, have kept this man, my son, from dying? Jesus wept.

The trip to the Grand Canyon, unbeknownst to me, would be a metaphor for my next trip, just a few weeks hence. Not all trips to the canyon serve the purpose of causing the two to become one. Not all draw one into the sense of awe and wonder that are often caused through seeing the magnificence of creation. Sometimes we stand on the rim, not to consecrate our oneness or to put ourselves in humble perspective before the vast beauty of our world. Sometimes we stand on the rim of the precipice instead to confront our own broken condition.

The canyons are really great beautiful scars carved into the face of the earth, revealing layer upon layer of life, lived and died, level upon level of evidence of past storms, of freezes and thaws, of blazing sun and tempestuous wind, of massive upheavals and enormous resettling, of compression and squeezing pressures, of massive forces cutting and slicing through living vegetation and layers of rock and soil, all of which combine to create the wondrous beauty we behold today. The beauty emerges through a furnace of natural affliction.

Grief is a master carver of canyons of all sorts in our lives. It slices and dices precious hopes, dreams, and aspirations. It presses the most loving of relationships into shapes never known before. The emotional strain is intense. We become forced to reach for one another over what seem to be vast distances, so vast that is easy to grow weary. We are repeatedly tempted to simply give up trying. Life goes on, but we're not sure why or if we care one way or another. We struggle with the malaise of indifference.

Chapter XXIV.

Marriage on the Brink, Fourteenth month AD

Someone I'd never met, a friend of my friend John, graciously agreed that we could use his house at Biddeford Pool on the southern coast of Maine during the week after Labor Day. We were grateful. John and Linda, Al and Nancy, dear friends all, came for a weekend during our stay. One night, we drank some wine, played some cards, and were simply enjoying one another's' company. The conversation was lively and veered into controversial topics. Everyone was growing increasingly passionate expressing their opinions.

Everyone, that is, except me. I was mute. Numb. I didn't feel a thing. I really didn't care to enter the fray. I was sitting ensconced in my emotional lethargy, when suddenly, all eyes came to my end of the table. "What do you think? Weigh in." Jean especially wanted me to rally to her point of view. The problem was that my usual spark for the topic or most anything else was totally dead. I had no opinion that I would be passionate about.

Jean experienced my lack of engagement as abandonment, touching an old wound from way back in her childhood. She felt forsaken and alone. I was defensive. I resented being expected to champion a position on issues that I really didn't care about at the time. Grief had gutted me but no one knew the extent of my emptiness. So all they could conclude was that I was a traitor, that I'd forsaken my passion for passivity. Grief had made me tentative and uncertain. My wife and my friends wanted more, but I did not have to offer what they wanted me to give. Finally we all said "Good night," but it was not a good night.

The next day our friends left for home, leaving Jean and me alone. I remember walking on the beach, and for the first time since way back in our teens, before we were married, I heard Jean wonder out loud if our relationship had come to an end, if we were finished as husband and wife. Our marriage was poised on the north rim of the grand canyon of destruction. Should we jump to the doom of our long marriage, or should we back away. It was a frightening and sobering moment.

Alone. This is the Bible's first "not good". "It is not good for the man to be alone." Genesis 2:18. Alone is one of the most intimidating faces of the void. The existentialist writers of the last century tried to have a staring contest with that face, to peer into the vast emptiness and not blink They concluded that life was absurd and that existence had no point beyond itself. If that is so, then grief is nothing at all save a grand illusion. So is love. So is any relationship that we deem meaningful. Life and the world cave in upon themselves and we are left having come full circle to the insights of the ancient preacher in Israel who said, "Vanity of vanities, all is vanity." (Ecclesiastes.)

Most of us believe that love is real, as is our grief and our hurt now. Human life is not pointless. Relationships of love matter. Our losses are significant. No matter how impenetrable are the questions concerning meaning and reasons which so persistently present themselves before us demanding answers and satisfaction of their demands, and no matter how impotent we are to supply what is demanded, still we cling to the notion that somewhere, somehow, things do make sense. That which we have cherished is not to be abandoned.

So we hold on to hope, even when all we feel is hopelessness. It is not for lack of courage, not because we can't face reality that we do this. At the core of our souls, we've been impregnated with a "yes" deeper than the barrage of "no's" which the void presents as the only logical explanations of ultimate reality. Faith, even in, or perhaps especially in the fiery furnace, keeps on saying yes, in spite of the heat and smoke that engulfs us when a child dies. Like Shadrach, Meshach, and Abednego, the three thrown into the fiery furnace in the Book of Daniel, when king void peers into the fire we are in, he sees another there with us. It may be the One whom we ourselves cannot even see. It is the presence of the Lord which finally is our only hope for survival.

As I've said before, grief is an isolating experience. I can remember resenting Jean for her grief because often it compounded my own. Here's how it went. I would finally be having a day with some brightness, some forgetfulness, some acknowledgment that after all God was good, my faith was still strong, and life was worth living. Then I would come home to find Jean in the pit of despair. And, in those moments, God forgive me, I would resent her. I resented her for stealing my little, hard won scrap of comfort and peace, for ruining my "good" day. I'm sure she had many similar times with me. She'd want to talk; I'd want to be silent. She'd worry about our finances, but I was grappling with sorrow and felt violated in being asked to think about it. I'd read something I found helpful, but couldn't share it because she was not receptive to ideas that I found comforting. She would trust, I would doubt. I would trust, she would doubt. The chasm between us was widening like an outgoing tide, leaving exposed the rotting detritus, the stinking emotional kelp, the empty spiritual shells that once were home to living insights and convictions, left lying in the damp mud of our wounded souls.

The tidal swing at Biddeford is dramatic. At low tide, large expanses of tidal land, a sort of mixture of sand and mud, are left exposed. We could walk to nearby islands that were surrounded by water when the tide came in. This was a natural metaphor for where we were at the time, alternating between being exposed and being hidden, washed but never really clean. Our grief clung to us like the leavings of low tide, like soap scum in a tub. We all grieve individually, personally, at our own pace. Each grief has a highly individualized timing and pace. My good days were incongruent with her bad days and vice versa. This easily becomes a breeding ground for resentment. Resentment fosters isolation.

Fortunately for us, we've grown up together, meeting at age 16. We have a history of surviving hard times. We are best of friends. We share a common faith, even under fire. But it's easy to see why so few marriages survive the loss of a child. The dynamics of this grief are powerful and relentless. It is not good for us to be alone, and yet, we are alone. Our sin and our sorrows, our suffering and disappointments, all are experienced at some deep level in our souls, privately and individually. Others may stand on the edge of the circle of our suffering and call our name; we can hear their voices, but they cannot enter in. Only the Lord has access to the deep things of our spirits. And when you feel God forsaken, it feels very much like you are there, in the suffering, abjectly alone. Even when faith and doctrine and scripture tell us that we will never be left alone nor forsaken, in the furnace of grief, such convictions are severely challenged.

It is not good for the man to be alone. It is not good for the woman either. So we backed away from the canyon rim of our own divorce and trudged onward into dark tomorrows, together in our aloneness.

Chapter XXV

Prayers for year II

Dear Lord, I am fighting for each ray of hope and looking to see light at the end of this endless tunnel. The months have crept as well as raced by. My grief seems as young as this morning's dawn and as old as the dawn of time, like it has always been with me. I have become convinced once more of your generous and continuous care for Jean and me. We still have so many questions and so much sorrow. At least now I have parts of each day that are not totally dominated by my sadness. Once in a while, I can forget, laugh, love, and enjoy my life. Thank you Lord for being so patient with me. As it has always been, so it is now; I don't deserve the kind of love you give. I am grateful that you give it anyway, not because of who I am, but because of who you are. I pray in Jesus' name. Amen.

O God, the numbness has officially worn off. It served to dull the force of my grief for the first year of the journey. Now I must trudge on with less between me and my loss. I do have the sense of your mercy through it all. I do believe Jon and we have been spared some very awful times. You know I would take him back in a minute if I thought we could prevail and see him set free down here. But believing as I do in the richness of glory where I am sure Jon is now, faced with the choice, I would not dare to bring him back.

That would be a choice only he could make. Of course it's moot. I surrender him to you, over and over and over, and the more I do, my grip on him grows weaker and weaker. I look forward to that day when I have totally given him over to you for eternity and until we meet again. Until then Lord, please accept my prayer. In your name I pray, Amen.

Lord Jesus Christ, Son of the living God, have mercy upon me, a sinner. Lord, my thoughts frighten me. I look into the void, not with courage but with mute despondency. Will this ever get better? Will I ever know joy again that is not haunted by sorrow? When shall I come again into your presence without these questions hanging in the air between us? Lord, please give me great forbearance. I know I speak rashly and foolishly from this hurting land. I would not be the accuser's apprentice, hurling angry blame in your direction. Help me to hold fast to my confidence in you and restore me to right standing, through Jesus I pray. Amen.

Jesus my redeemer, I arise today to greet the dawn and begin another day. I don't know what will meet me. Will it be a day filled with sorrow, or a day with some periods of relief, with islands of normal feelings to dot the landscape of grief? I am finding it so hard to get a sense that I am pleasing you with my living. I get so mired in the confusion caused by my loss. I am trying to be courageous in facing it. I know it is not good to avoid the pain. I feel guilty when my acrimony spews in your direction. And I am afraid that in my presumption I will cross some line between us and not be able to get back to you. Nevertheless, I believe you hold me fast, you understand my struggle, and you will never let me go. I love you Lord and am clinging to the hem of your garment, awaiting the flow of your healing power to come in my direction. Receive my prayer in your name and for your sake, Lord Jesus Christ. Amen.

Chapter XXVI

Fifteenth Month AD: Sabbatical Granted

J on died on July 23rd, 2005. Later that year, I discovered the existence of sabbatical grants offered to pastors from the Lilly Endowment. I was moved to apply. The application process required that a detailed plan be developed. The literature advised that applicants pursue that which made their hearts sing. A considerable sum of money would be awarded and the congregation was expected to release me from duty for four months. It was a long and thorough process but I decided to go for it. It was a challenge because the only songs my heart was singing at the time were lamentations.

This became an exercise in looking somewhere out beyond my sorrow. Where *would* I want to go if I were free of this paralysis for a time? If I could do anything I wanted and had the funds to do it, what would it be? I would have to cultivate hope once again. I would have to risk giving myself to expectations which could easily be disappointed. It would require much effort. Would it be worth it? I had to fight through it all, all the questions, fears, doubts, and the atrophy of my soul caused by sorrow.

Jean had no apparent interest and no expectation of success. She was in no shape to risk hope. I was on my own, alone. So I began to dream and a plan began to emerge. I determined that what was most important to me were my relationships with family and with friends. And since travel was to be included, I decided I wanted to go where there would be no language barrier with which to contend, so the British Isles fit the bill. I wrote up my portion of the plan seeking to focus on these priorities. A small team of lay people from my church wrote up what they proposed for the congregation to do in my absence. They united and expressed their support for me. On the wings of a prayer, I dropped my proposal in the mail in May of 2006.

At the beginning of the fifteenth month after Jon died, I received confirmation through the mail that I had been awarded the grant. Kathy, my secretary, called me at home and said that a large white envelope had arrived at church and she thought I might want to come see what was in it. I drove nervously to pick it up. Holding the envelope in my hands, poised to rip it open and get the verdict, there was truly a mixture of sheer adrenaline and near terror. So much for me was riding on the contents. Was it yes or was it no? When I opened it and saw that the grant had been awarded I was flooded with excitement and joy unlike any I had experienced for a very long time.

For the first time since Jon's death I thought I saw a dent in Jean's armor plated grief. There was a glimmer of life there, under the emotional flat line. A heart beat showed up on the monitor. There was hope after all. It was finally beginning to dawn on me that God was lavishly showering me with healing love.

Strangely, I felt too that the grant was a gift from Jon. When I wrote my proposal, I mentioned that we had lost a son and were looking for a time away from ministry to heal and be renewed. I tried not to overplay our tragedy, but simply included it in my narrative. I am guessing that my request found favor because the review committee was moved to compassion because of our loss. I in turn have been moved to great gratitude to the Lord and to the Lilly Endowment, and to Jon, for a gift that continues to bless me long afterward.

The ending of the Book of Job began to make a little more sense to me. After Job lost everything, except the shrill voice of his wife who encouraged him to curse God and die, God arrived, silenced the foolish and cruel counselors, blew him away with questions of His own, without any attempt to explain Job's calamities, and began to simply shower him with blessings. These were not replacements for what was lost. His children were irreplaceable. But somehow, the lavish kindness of God enabled him to move forward in living his life.

Some scholars believe that the Book of Job is a pastoral allegory written to address the nation of Israel in exile. They see it as an attempt to speak to Israel of their faith and hope in God, and to silence the false explanations which misrepresent God and explain their sufferings by assigning blame. In extreme misfortune it is all too tempting for people to begin ferreting around amidst the shards of life, peering through the tears of suffering people to find an explanation which exonerates God and faith and finds fault with the victims. To this, God says an emphatic "No!"

Losing a child is like being dragged off into exile. Home as you know it becomes a shattered place. Relationships strain and often tear apart. Simple pleasures and common routines become dull and lifeless. You lose your native language; the things you used to say and mean no longer mean the same thing to you and you may find yourself retreating into a painful silence. Cherished beliefs may come to sound foolish in your ears. Old assumptions upon which you have built your life before your loss may seem to tumble down like a house of cards. Time alone will not heal the devastation. It takes more power to withstand this onslaught than you can muster by yourself. It takes a deeper concern than your family and friends alone can offer. It takes the power and love of a mighty God to bring restoration to the heart of a parent who has lost a child.

Chapter XXVII

Journeys of Restoration

Journal Entry: April 24th, 2007

In July it will be two years. Lately, the grief has felt nothing short of resurgent for both Jean and me. The signs of God's love since Jon's death have been extravagant! We've had free trips to San Diego, the Grand Canyon, the coast of Maine, and now my four month sabbatical. And there have been many smaller signs of God blessing us. We've not been able to be as grateful as we should; all of our responses to God's kindness get pressed through the sieve of our brokenness. We've been angry at God and others. We've had trouble trusting, hoping, and even believing. Under all the emotional and spiritual turmoil our faith has remained as the bedrock of our existence. With the disciples we say, "To whom shall we go Lord. You have the words of eternal life." God has been patient and long suffering with us. I know he knows what we're going through. My sabbatical begins in less than three weeks.

The "why" questions are unanswerable and even if the intellect were satisfied, our hearts would not be satisfied, would still be broken. "The heart has reasons that the reason knows not of" is how Pascal put it. Why didn't God step in and spare Jon according to our prayers? Why didn't God exercise his goodness according to our "wise" plan and requested outcome?

Why? And the "How" questions, the "Why" questions' kissing cousins, made the scene. How could a good God allow this? How can we ever again trust a god who would allow this? And so on and on it goes.

God is not beholden to our demands for sense to be made, for reasons to be given, not if God doesn't want to or deem it to be wise. God proceeds according to God's own counsel. The how and why questions never have been answered, perhaps because they were not the right questions in the first place. Perhaps God was working in a way that transcended such questions even though they presented themselves with such demanding force. Instead of catering to my insistent demands for reasons, God instead seemed to open a tap somewhere and grace and mercy began to flow in my direction, or more accurately, I began to be aware of these things that had I been able to see more clearly would have been seen to be flowing all the time. I was just too lost in sadness to be that aware, at least until this point. Receiving the Lilly grant proved to be a tipping point for me.

The month of May arrived slowly. Goodbyes were said and prayers were offered by my congregation on our behalf as my sabbatical finally got under way. Four months of restoration began. We started with a week in Ocean City, New Jersey, given for free by our dear friends from New Hampshire, Al and Nancy. We had met years ago at a renewal event for a congregation in upstate New York for which I was the preacher and they were members of the visiting team of lay people who had come to serve. At the time, they were in a great deal of pain themselves and God knitted our hearts together in a fast and lasting friendship as we shared in love and prayer.

It was Al and Nancy who travelled from New Hampshire to our home in southern New Jersey that first Christmas after Jon died to help us set up and decorate our Christmas tree. They were thoughtful and perceptive enough to know what a hard time we were about to experience. They were generous enough to give of themselves in a tangible gift of mercy. It was an amazing and loving gift that really touched our hearts.

This precious time together has become a tradition in the years since that first sad December. We have marveled each year as they continue to leave home to come be with us, as early December marks the onset of a season where we all get extra busy with our own holiday preparations. They put their lives on the line for us over and over. This sort of gift is so precious to those walking through such a durable sorrow.

The mid-May weather in Ocean City was cool and breezy that year and we had a wonderful relaxing week together. Al and Nancy were so easy to be with because they had no frantic need to be entertained. They had no compulsion to tour the area. We read, walked, talked, sang, prayed, ate good food, and shared life together during our stay. Again we were immensely grateful as the love of good friends washed over our hearts. It was the perfect beginning to my sabbatical.

The second week, I was offered a free cabin in the Pocono Mountains of Pennsylvania by a fellow pastor. My oldest son Mark, himself a Presbyterian pastor, and I headed off together for a week of father and son time, to pray, to walk, to share, to be together without any real agenda. We spoke of Jon's death and how it was affecting us. It was helpful for me to connect with the wounds carried by my son. Our time together was creating another small crack in the armor-plated face of the void named "alone."

Andrew's place was a rustic old farmhouse with a cozy family room encased in many windows which looked out on a large expanse of field which had once been a potato farm. Bird feeders hung from a huge old hemlock tree. I filled them with seed and waited for the show which didn't take long to begin. I watched and identified numerous species of birds, including a small flock of cedar waxwings which I identified after looking them up in the Audubon book which I found on the shelf. We saw some wild turkeys, red tailed hawks, and white tailed deer. We both painted a little with our watercolors. We took a long walk along a nearby railroad bed, now converted to a cinder path along the Lehigh River and talked some about Jon.

Neither Mark nor Julia has spoken much to me about their grief, which is a bit of a mystery to me for which I don't know the reason. I have my questions. Do they think of him as often as I do? What sort of emotions are they dealing with and how intense are they? I send them signals that I am open to discuss things, but they don't seem to be too eager to do so. I try for my part to be respectful and resist pushing my way into a place that they would rather not open. I wish there was some way I could help them along.

On the way home we stopped to see old friends Lou and Linda on their farm in the Lehigh Valley, and Mark was "wowed" by Lou's timber frame house, a live-in work of art. I myself spent a few work days helping with the construction and have a small measure of pride in the finished product.

Lou was given an old barn, free for the dismantling and hauling away of the timbers. He noted and catalogued the marked beams and eventually reconstructed the structure to serve as the great room in the middle of two adjoining wings of the house, one for sleeping quarters, and one for a large country kitchen. I sensed some longing awakening in Mark, who is after all the son of a dome builder himself, and thought maybe someday he would buy some land and either build or rehabilitate a home too.

It strikes me now that rebuilding my life after the destruction, the dismantling caused by Jon's death, is a process akin to what Lou did with the old barn beams. Each beam was marked with a number supplying the code which guided the initial construction so long ago, and still served as a guide for the reconstruction. The beams of my trust in God, my faith, my theology, remained sound. In the end, most still fit together. They show some of the signs of the distress sustained through long years of service and the fires of testing, but they still will support a substantial structure. They get new siding, new wiring, new plumbing, new insulation, a new roof, but the framework is proven and still strong. There is a rugged beauty in such a life that is lacking in one still untested and unproven. New wings are added but there is gold in these old beams.

After a fine farm-style lunch, Mark and I made our way back south to our eagerly awaiting wives and his children. It had been a good few days for me. My hope was that Mark would see clearly how much I love him and how much I valued spending time with him and how proud of him I am. The sudden death of someone you love should put you on alert that tomorrow is a gift not guaranteed.

My advice to any and all who will receive it is this. It is wise to live up to date. Tell someone you love them. Make contact and don't put it off. Do not assume that there will be time later. All tomorrows come as a gift. Do not live presuming that you will have an endless supply. Everyone who lives has a day sooner or later that is next to the last. If you knew this was your next to the last day, how would you spend it? To whom would you speak? With whom would you seek to make amends and be reconciled? Whom would you thank? What would you give away? Facing our mortality is not morbid; facing it is both focusing and freeing. It helps us avoid ending our life with a pile of regrets over missed opportunities.

Shortly after my week with Mark, Jean and I travelled to see Randy and Donna in Goochland, Virginia, where we stayed for free in a small timber framed guest house owned by a friend of Randy's named Lewis S. The cabin was itself another work of the timber framer's art with exquisite details in wood, stone, and wrought iron. The timbers here were not reclaimed from an older structure but were newly hand hewn. It felt like a one man version of a great cathedral made in miniature. It was situated on the edge of a small, man-made lake and surrounded by the woods.

Lewis runs a concrete and stone business in Richmond so he owned enough heavy equipment to accomplish many heavy tasks in his spare time. One such project was the small but beautiful lake that lay at our door. I asked what sort of permits he had to get to build the lake and he replied in his typically droll way that it is always better to leave the government out of things whenever possible. On his property he followed a "don't ask, don't tell" policy.

When it comes to personal business and bureaucrats I couldn't agree more. I know how many years it took just to convince the IRS that Jon was no longer alive and they were going to have a very hard time collecting the back taxes they said he owed. For over four years, even after numerous letters informing the government that Jon was deceased, sending them more than one official death certificate, I kept getting bills addressed to Jon for taxes owed. They were mildly painful and upset Jean each time they came. I finally began to draw a line through the name and address, write "deceased" on the envelope, and send them back unopened.

Lewis and his wife showed us warm Virginia hospitality and invited us to a country feast in their home atop the hill from where we were staying. It too is a large and exquisite timber framed structure, again complemented by equal artistry in granite, marble and wrought iron. Friends and family all gathered for a lovely summer evening of food and fellowship. Large surrounding decks looked out through the gentle Virginia woods and down upon the Rivanna River which meandered below.

The steaks were prime and grilled outside over charcoal, the baked potatoes the size of small watermelons (forgive the hyperbole), fresh corn and tomatoes, green beans, and a huge salad. There was fresh pie and ice cream for dessert. It was country fare fit for a king. As afternoon faded into evening, the quality of this gathering into which we had been so graciously received felt almost magical.

The following day was Pentecost and we traveled to Jamestown and attended the noon prayer service at the oldest church in the United States. At the start of the day I was feeling a mild remorse that I would not be in worship on Pentecost, so "stumbling" upon this opportunity felt like a divinely arranged opportunity, which in fact, I believe it was. It was very moving to be there. The service was simple and bare boned, just what we needed at the time. The prayers from the Anglican prayer book were elegant and deep rooted. I had a taste of my own personal Pentecost in this historic setting as I once again sensed the kind Spirit hovering over the waters of my inner chaos and saying, "Peace. Be still."

From there we went over to colonial Williamsburg and walked around, touring the old historic church where so many of our founding fathers worshipped regularly. Again, I felt as though I was being put in touch with an old root system that carried real strength and comfort in my direction.

The day after that was Memorial Day and we took a canoe float down the Rivanna River from Lewis's landing to the confluence of the Rivanna and the James Rivers. The float was relaxing and enjoyable. The Rivanna is not very deep, probably averaging one to four feet in depth in most places and flows along at a good clip so not much paddling is required. Just below I could see different varieties of fish swimming along under our canoe. There were bass and various pan fish, suckers, minnows and gar. Suddenly we roused a bald eagle that flew from just yards ahead of us downriver and out of sight. And I heard the voice of the Lord enter my thoughts and say, "You are afloat on a river of sadness. Don't be afraid. Just as you don't control the flow of the river or the flight of the eagle, this gentle river and this great bird are signs that I am with you and am out ahead to chart your course and to watch over you." It was only the second eagle I had ever seen in the wild, the first being the one I saw at the site of Big Joe's death so many years ago.

It was on a family camping trip for Jean and me and our three small children. We had wandered in our camper across northwestern Pennsylvania, looking unsuccessfully for a suitable camp site. We ended up in a KOA campground in Bellefonte, just north of State College. I got the distinct impression that I should revisit the site of Big Joe's fatal fall. Even though it had been many years since I'd been there, I thought I could find it and sure enough I did. I was experiencing great apprehension as we approached, going down the slope to the small saddle of land where I had camped so many years before with my college friends. My fears grew stronger as we walked up the gentle incline to the top of the cliff where Joe had taken his last flight into eternity.

There on the spot was now a small railing of steel pipes set in concrete with a memorial marker in memory of someone else's son who had fallen to his death. I was very nervous as my children had no healthy fear and no respect for this calamitous edge overlooking Spruce Creek. I made them sit close. Then there it came, my first ever bald eagle sighting. The majestic eagle flew by, at eye level. It seemed as though he was looking right into my soul. I can't explain it but it was a healing vision. It was as though God were saying, "I saw what happened here so long ago. I see you now. All is well. I will never remove my watchful gaze from your life." My next eagle sighting would be many years later, the one mentioned above, as we canoed down the Rivanna River nearly two years after Jon's death.

My point in telling you these things is not to bore you with slides of my vacation but to notice with you two things. First note the recurrence of the word free. I have not even mentioned places freely given by my longtime dentist and friend, John G. whose cabin in Conway in the heart of the White Mountains of New Hampshire supplied us with a beautiful haven for rest and refreshment. Then there is the old, sprawling vacation house in Lincolnville Beach, just north of the quaint village of Camden on the mid-coast of Maine, belonging to Karen R, who I had met on a preaching mission, again freely offered and gratefully received. And then there is the place given for me and my family to use by parishioners Frank and Roberta H. in the Pocono Mountains of Pennsylvania. Or how about the beach house in Avalon, New Jersey, freely and repeatedly offered to me in the off season by my dear friend Gerry O., the place where much of this writing has been done and where many a prayer retreat has been taken by Jean and me? I have more offers than I have time to accept. You are probably thinking that I am a typical free-loading clergyman! That I am. I am a free-loader of Grace! God uses real people to deliver the blessings God intends as reminders of just how much God loves us.

Grief is binding and constricting. It makes the soul feel impoverished, depleted, tired and worn out. The love of God comes freely and lavishly and sets us free. Over and over and over blessings of all sorts arrive with no strings attached. Please do not misunderstand me here. The Lord was not trying with gifts to compensate me for the loss I had sustained. That would be an insult to God and to me. Jon had died. Neither reason nor gift would justify or diminish the pain of that loss. God was and is simply doing what God always does whether or not I am in any condition or suitable frame of mind and heart to receive from God. God is pouring love and blessings in my direction because like John, I am "the disciple whom Jesus loves" and is God's nature to bless his children.

When abundant grace meets a wounded soul, the result is healing. This process of the restoration of our souls finds its outlet in gratitude for grace. The antidote for the anger and disappointment we feel toward God lies in the restoration of our capacity to feel gratitude and once again begin to live thankfully. Thanksgiving begins slowly but persistently to melt the icebergs of bitterness that clog the arteries of life and threaten to sink our hearts under their prodigious weight.

Secondly, let me underline the fact noted above that the gifts that arrive freely, though sometimes mystical in nature like the surprise sightings of an eagle, more often than not are firmly rooted in the hearts and are delivered by the hands of the people in our world. They may be people that we do not know, or people that we have known and loved for many years.

I saw the love of God's heart working through the unknown hands and hearts that awarded to me my sabbatical grant. I thought with gratitude of the philanthropic intention of the Lilly family who many years ago set up the foundation that is now used annually to further religion in American life. The responsibility for administering the fund has passed down through the decades to the group that selected my proposal out of a stack of hundreds of applications from other pastors, no doubt all deserving and in need of the blessing. I simply felt the Lord whispering to me, no, more like shouting, "I know how badly you are hurting and I want you to know how much I love you!"

The love we receive, the care, the kindness, the compassion, show up through real people with real lives and with real troubles all their own but who are still motivated to expend themselves on our behalf. Our part and our challenge is to be open enough to receive their gifts in a season where our instinct may be to close ourselves off from all forms of risk which is an inevitable component of all real relationships. It is hard to be blessed and play it safe all at once. It is a battle worth fighting, to hold yourself as open as you can to the operations of grace which invade the pit with healing light from many different sources. The light that shines there will cause the gold to glint and gleam enough to catch our eyes and enrich us if we are willing to live with open eyes and hearts.

Chapter XXVIII

Grace in Great Britain

The centerpiece of my sabbatical was our five week trip through England, Scotland, and Ireland, just the two of us, Jean and myself, mostly in bed and breakfast lodgings, mostly in a small car, with lots of walking and some train rides thrown in for good measure. I had spent months and months researching and planning our itinerary and booking accommodations far in advance. Jean seemed to take no interest at the time, since she really didn't believe the grant would be awarded. Attempts to involve her in the process were fended off with a pronounced lack of enthusiasm.

I was unaccustomed to working on such a major project without Jean's partnership, but I forged ahead and made a plan. I prayed my way through the work, seeking the Lord's guidance and wisdom that I needed. I studied guidebooks and spent many hours on the internet doing research and making reservations. The Lord blessed this all in such minute detail that even I was not so thick as to miss a very loving hand at work.

We landed in Gatwick airport south of London and took the train into the city, disembarking at Waterloo Station. We found our first lodging place just a few blocks away, right next to the huge Ferris wheel known as the eye of London, sitting on the bank of the Thames opposite Westminster. For the next five weeks we followed our noses, meandering from point to point according to the plan I had made.

Miraculously, for a trip planned by a total novice like myself, the journey went flawlessly from beginning to end. We spent every waking hour and hours not awake, in very close quarters. Jean was a courageous good sport as I learned to drive on the "wrong" side of the road. She and a German tourist we met in a pub in Kinsale, Ireland, agreed that riding with their husbands on the left hand side of the road was a bit like sitting in the dentist's chair, tightly gripping the arms in anticipation of the pain about to be inflicted.

During the days and weeks of this wonderful journey we discovered anew what good friends and mates we are. The grief had not destroyed us after all. We had endured and overcome much and were once again drawing closer together. Sharing what for us was a great adventure helped us to remember how much we cherished one another. What a relief!

Chapter XXIX

Another Anniversary
and Some Old Wisdom

Journal Entry, Monday, July 23rd, the second anniversary of Jon's death.

Dear Jon,

It's been a long time since I wrote. Mom and I have been running all over England, Scotland, Wales, and Ireland, filling our eyes with beauty, feeling the healing ministry of God for our souls, but always carrying the pain of losing you. We've each tucked you away, along with most of our pain, in some secret recess of our hearts. Of course it's not a tame sorrow, nor a very well hidden secret. Every once in a while the grief erupts like a volcano spewing a hot lava flow of tears, but most days it just seeps like a spring that never dries up.

We see young men who remind us of you, or beach scenes, or it could be anything really that acts as a trigger for our memories, some sweet and some painful. For the longest time there was nothing but the pain, but few can live without respite, so we're learning to make room once again for joys and pleasures. Most of them are tempered now though with our loss. I was wondering this morning as I awoke; will you have regrets until we meet again, sort of like a purgatory of sorrow until mutual amends can be made between us. I actually hope that's not the case. You've suffered enough already and so have we.

I have no idea how many of my sins were visited upon you, or how many of my father's and grandfathers' have been visited upon me and you. We'd both be surprised I guess. And the sins of the children boomerang back on the parents as well and club them where they are most vulnerable, in their love for their children.

This is the second anniversary of your death, of your home going, of the Troubles. Here in Ireland, "The troubles" refers to the period of violent clashes between Protestants and Catholics. Obviously I'm using it in a far different manner. It has been such a difficult journey for all of us who have loved you and who love you still. We all feel cheated by your departure. We've resolutely tried to see God's mercy in it too, but that's been an exercise in blind trust and very much an uphill battle. We don't know what you were to become as a mature man, but to all of us it seemed that your life held special promise. Not that you weren't already someone special. You always were! Your name means "God has given," and you are God's gift to us.

It is especially hard for me to see your mom's grief. I've tried to be kind to her and patient, at which I sometimes have failed, being frayed as I am by my own hurt. I regret that you never got to experience a long term, faithful love for a mate, though I'm sure where you are love and fidelity are not in short supply.

We never know how our days will unfold, but we're expecting a grief day on this anniversary. I'll live it with mom as our travels continue. We both love you dear son. Until we meet, much love, Dad.

Journal Entry, July 24ᵗʰ, 2007

We had a pretty strong grief day yesterday. We called home and talked to Julia and the kids. She had a hard, sad day as well. Strange to say, the day was also magnificent.

As I edit this 21 months later, in April of 2009, I realize in hindsight that this combination of grief and restoration to joy in life was quite significant. A new balance had begun to emerge between my sorrow and the rest of my life, though I didn't know it so consciously then as I do now. I was just living with the contradictions with little attempt to explain how they fit together. It was enough to get through the day and find whatever consolation was there to be had.

The drive around the Dingle peninsula was everything I'd hoped for and more. Vistas of rugged yet somehow gentle beauty lay around every turn. Our first stop, other than our pauses at every little turn out to gaze at cliffs pounded relentlessly by Atlantic surf, was at some ancient beehive huts on a very old stone enclosed farmstead. The artistry in stone, everywhere apparent in all the British Isles, was on elegant but rugged display here.

The views got progressively more dramatic until we got to Slea Head, which was simply fantastic. We climbed atop this grass and bracken covered head of land with its large standing stone at the summit and an old WWII concrete watch station. The granite outcroppings, Skellig Michael and Little Skellig rose from the ocean to our south, and to the north we could see the Great Blaskett Island. We descended to a sheltered cove just below Slea Head and Jean took off her shoes and waded in the cold surf. The sea water was clear with vivid shades of viridian and deep greens and blues. The weather was sunny (a condition worth noting in Ireland) and a cool wind blew.

Back on the road, we headed north and decided to stop at the Blaskett Island Exhibition Center, which my first impulse was to skip but I decided that at the least I should use the rest room since I didn't know what facilities were available between here and Tralee, our next destination for the night's lodging. Surprisingly, this stop turned out to be one of the highlights of our trip. I found the story of the hearty people who inhabited the Great Blaskett Island until 1953 when the government forced *them to resettle on the mainland compelling. All the younger people had either died or escaped the austere island existence for life in America, leaving the community decimated and the elderly to fend for themselves until they simply could no longer sustain their rugged village surrounded by such extremely harsh conditions. The exhibition eloquently keeps their story alive. There was a moving display of oil paintings by Irish artist Carol Cronin. I sat for some considerable time absorbing the visual and emotional impact of her vivid artistry. I purchased several volumes of stories authored by the old Blaskett Island storytellers, <u>An Old Woman's Reflections</u>, by Peig Sayers and <u>A Pity Youth Does Not Last</u>, by Micheal O'Guiheen.*

I became instantly enamored with these simple and rugged Blaskett Island writers, their stories, poems, and prayers. Early in the last century, some scholars discovered this little enclave of people in this island village who still spoke pure Gaelic Irish. They set out to capture this language and the lore of its speakers before it became altogether extinct. Their writings embody that distinct blend of melancholy and mirth that, in my mind at least, is quintessentially Irish. I found a deep resonance in my own soul with this amalgam of opposites. I was, and still am, infatuated with and admiring of the rugged courage and unique community that was inherent in the culture among the dwellers on the Great Blaskett Island. The community eventually died by attrition as one after another their young people escaped to radically easier lives on the mainland and in America. When the government finally moved the remaining islanders to the mainland in the 1950s, all that remained were the ruins of their humble cottages on the island, and the rich literature of their storytellers and poets.

I wonder if the old timers felt something akin to the loss I feel as they lost their youth and then their community to the wide world. Some, like me, lost their young ones due to the dangers of living in such harsh conditions. Maybe it was better to see others make their escape to a more tame and prosperous life.

Whatever the case, I wonder if it felt to them as it does now to me, as though their future had been stolen.

Unlike me, some, though not all, could imagine their young ones still alive in this world pursuing a better life in a far away land. My son too is far away, but I am not able to visit nor am I able to call him up and hear his voice. I don't get letters home saying, "All is well. Wish you were here." Jon's death made me feel old and isolated before my time. I tried to hold on to the island of my former existence, the time before I became a father who has lost a child, but the effort was futile. Life as I knew it has been snatched away never to return. Growing old often feels like this I guess.

Listen to one of the reflections of Peig Sayers:

"The long years are gone in a gallop, and these who are in the life of my story gone too, as the mist goes with the wind. I can see today only the place where they used to live, but they draw me back on the lonely road of thoughts, and 'tis nice how Youth pays me a small visit, when I'm at tight grips with the years. I am young again, I think. There is courage and merriment in my heart. I feel the mind as strong and courageous as ever it was. But when the fine pleasant thoughts go, rust and sourness and weakness of the brain comes on me and I feel some heavy weight coming down on my heart.

Maybe the reader has youth in power. If so, he feels the heart light and secure, the laugh clean, the jump musical, the jollity and merriment, the brightness and freshness and fragrance everywhere on his way. I remember having all those little jewels myself, but see how the ugly thief age came and stole them from me! Great as the guarding is, he sneaks upon us. Nobody feels him coming." [3]

As we age, we accumulate things until we come to the point where we want to lighten our load again and divest ourselves of the burdens and responsibilities that come with possessions. We strive to simplify our lives and get our affairs in order. We gain wisdom along the way if we are paying attention. We gain breadth and perspective. We learn humility and compassion. We learn to sift through life and identify the things that matter and to distinguish them from the things that don't. Losing a child accelerates this process to a dizzying speed. We may become blinded, thinking that things which do matter don't, and thinking that things that don't matter do. We pass through a dark tunnel of radical displacement and disorientation. We need help to recover our hard-won faith and hope.

Feel the simple and direct power of this prayer of Micheal O'Guiheen:

"O God of Grace, Whose goodness is without end, grant us to love You in this life, so as nothing would be coming between ourselves and You that would make You have disgust and hatred for us. For all this life will come to nothing and all that will be there will be You, O God of truth and right, in Whom we put all our trust and hope. Be merciful to us, O Lord God, and guide our path in this vale of tears. Do not let that foul enemy who travels through this life lead us astray....Praise and thanks to You, O Lord God, when the need is greatest, that is when you are nearest to us.....Is it not well I know Your Holy help, O Lord, for it was often I was held in the grip of black clouds of sorrow and no way out for me except Your help. I have this much to say, that God helps the weak and gives us peace of mind." Micheal O'Guiheen [4]

Oh old man of the Great Blaskett Island, how well and wisely put: "when the need is greatest, that is when you are nearest to us." Lord, be near all of us who need you now so desperately.

From there we finished the loop around the Dingle Peninsula and headed up through Connor's Pass, threaded our way down the needle thin and switch backed road heading north, and on to the small workaday city of Tralee in western Ireland. We checked into our high ceilinged room at the bed and break-fast and went out to walk around the city. We had pizza at a small place on the city square. Young people hanging out, some with skateboards, were a reminders of Jon on this, the second anniversary of his death, reminders of the son we had lost for good. After a leisurely stroll through the impressive city park with its extensive and beautiful rose gardens, a sculpture garden, and its monument in honor of Rose Kennedy, hometown girl made good, the sadness put us to bed that night and we fell into the mercy of sleep.

Chapter **XXX**

Gold on the Shore

Our trip was a wonder on many different levels for many different reasons, touching heart longings of all sorts in me that seemed to be deeply embedded from childhood, perhaps even before childhood in ancestral roots and trans-generational memories. Of all the British Isles, there was something gripping for me about the Emerald Isle, emotionally and spiritually, something that I still can't explain, so I'll leave it at that.

But I will beg your indulgence as I recount one personal encounter that I had in Portrush, a declining coastal resort on the very northern coast of Ireland. We had only a few days left before we headed back south to catch our flight home from Dublin.

It happened at sunset about 10:30 one evening. It was one of the only times I was not with Jean who had chosen to go to our room and turn in after a very long day. Had she been with me what was about to transpire most likely would not have happened.

I was unable to resist staying out to photograph and witness what promised to be a dramatic sunset over the North Atlantic. Waves crashed over rocks and a cool wind blew against my face. I scrabbled out upon a promontory of boulders to be as close to the edge of things as I could. The sunset was indeed glorious. As I returned to the beach in the fading light, a rather plain looking woman was seated alone, also watching. We exchanged pleasantries, and "wasn't it lucky that the rain had stopped so we could see this?", and "no I didn't believe in luck, being a man of faith." In an instant a door opened and we discovered that we both knew the Lord.

Then she opened a window in her soul to me and the conversation became a jewel studded interaction between pilgrims. Her name was Marian. She told me she had lost a child by a miscarriage. Emboldened by my comment that I too had lost a child, she shared that it was on the nearby cliff where I had been shortly before, a place of majestic beauty, it was there she had seriously contemplated taking her own life by throwing herself upon the rocks below. The death of her baby had shattered her to the point of despair. She was encountered at just that moment of decision by an old man's little dog who raced up to her, and laid his head on her foot and gazed up tenderly at her face. Then she heard a voice inside say, "Marian, don't do this."

The next day, she met, seemingly by chance, a minister who invited her for a conversation over a cup of tea. He helped her give her heart to Christ. The unbeatable combination in the British Isles, tea and the Holy Spirit; who can withstand such a duo of graciousness and Grace!

I told her my story and Jon's, and she shared deeply of her own experience. She wondered out loud, apologetically for being so personal, how it was that we were conversing at such a deep level, being perfect strangers as we were. I said I didn't mind at all. It was gold shining through in the fellowship of suffering. Finally, we parted ways. "I'll see you in heaven" said I. "Safe home," said she, which has become a personal favorite Irish colloquialism of mine ever since. Safe home. That is the point, when all is said and done.

Chapter XXXI

Safe home

A few days later, we were safe home. We flew out of Dublin on a partly cloudy morning, traveling west over Ireland bound for Philadelphia. We were not far into the flight as we neared the west coast which I had so quickly grown to love. Amazingly, the sky was clear and there I could see Skellig Michael and Little Skellig and the Great Blaskett Island, those little outcroppings of rock which summoned up for me the lines from St. Patrick's Breastplate: "I bind to myself today the virtues of the starlit heaven, the glorious sun's life-giving ray, the whiteness of the moon at even, the flashing of the lightning free, the whirling wind's tempestuous shocks, the stable earth, the deep salt sea, around the old eternal rocks." The old eternal rocks pounded relentlessly by the waves of endless stormy seas and yet enduring signaled me a strong farewell.

There on the plane I cried many tears of gratitude and of longing to return with no attempt to stem their flow. I had been given a parting glimpse of a fulfillment of the words of Jesus; "If these were silent, even the rocks would cry out." Even in this God was touching me, heart and soul, high above the Emerald Isle. I will not be silent Lord. I will yet praise you, my rock and my redeemer!

Shortly thereafter, Jean and I were home and out for a walk around our neighborhood, reflecting on our trip. She said, "The trip showed me that it was okay to have fun again." I can't remember any words ever that were more welcome and more touching and more restorative. My beloved mate was showing real signs of emerging from the dark places. But of course the work of grief was far from over. But at least, it was changing. What I had come to hope for and to expect was to not be stuck. I was fighting to keep a certain fluid quality to my sorrowing. I conceptualized the task as living with an evolving sorrow. And most importantly to me, my partner in life was being restored to me in ever deepening ways. In fact, the depth of our union began to go deeper than ever before. That deepening has continued on until this day.

Chapter XXXII

More Beach Music

For the last big bash of my sabbatical leave, I rented a large house in Kennebunk Beach on the Maine coast, just south of the spot of our marital low point a year earlier at Biddeford Pool. The house was a block from the beach and big enough to house us, along with Mark and Julia and their families. It was a memorable two weeks. We laughed, sang, ate lobster, walked, explored the tidal pools, watched grandchildren, all five of them, went on a whale watch, and did whatever our vacationers' hearts desired.

Al and Nancy and their family were staying just to the south at York Beach and their daughter Lisa and son-in-law Brendan wanted me to help them renew their wedding vows. They wanted me to play my guitar and sing them a song during the ceremony. I consented and knew just the song. The difficulty lay in the fact that the song I was moved to give as a gift to them was "In Your Eyes" written by Peter Gabriel:

Love, I get so lost sometimes. Days pass, and this emptiness
   fills my heart.
When I want to run away, I drive off in my car.
But whichever way I go, I come back to the place that you are
And all my instincts, they return. And the grand façade, so soon
   will burn;

Without a noise, without my pride, I reach out from the inside.

In your eyes, the light and the heat, I am complete
I see the doorways to a thousand churches
And resolution of all my fruitless searches
I want to touch the light the heat I see in your eyes, in your eyes.

It was another song that Jon had urged me to learn so I could teach it to him. I tried unsuccessfully right up to the end of his life. It was another anthem of my grief that I struggled to play through many tears. It also was quite painful for Jean since he had shared it with her as a personal favorite. I sought her permission to perform it for Lisa and Brendan as I did not want to commit an emotional ambush on her. After careful consideration, Jean consented. I hadn't been singing and playing too much at the time, but this song I felt I could deliver with deep passion.

Love, I don't like to see so much pain.
So much wasted, and each moment is slipping away.
I get so tired, working so hard for our survival
So I look to these times with you, to keep me awake and alive.
And all my instincts, they return.
And the grand facade so soon will burn
Without a noise, without my pride, I reach out from the inside.

Oh, oh, oh; in your eyes, the light and the heat, I am complete
I see the doorways to a thousand churches
And resolution of all my fruitless searches
I want to touch the light the heat I see in your eyes
Yes I want to be that complete; I want to touch the light the heat I see
In your eyes, in your eyes. [5]

I got through it. I spoke to them of the difficulties of being well wed over the long haul, of the process of inner healing for the wounds we sustain along the way, of the light and the heat, not only in one another's eyes, but the faithful and healing light in the eyes of Christ that is always with us and for us.

As the bright, sunny day gave way to dusk and then dark, the memories of my sorrow and the joy of our friends' celebration mingled together forming a fine snapshot of how life could once again become filled with love and friendship that would not be overwhelmed by sorrow, even though the sadness mingled in with the gladness. We sang and feasted on lobsters atop the bluff overlooking York beach. We could hear the waves incessant crashing below. We could see the lights of the town come to life for another night. There was good conversation and lots of warm hearted affection among friends old and new. It was like a little oasis in the midst of a vast sea of trouble.

"I get so tired, working so hard for our survival." This lyric still raises the haunting specter in my mind of the last months of Jon's life, of the ongoing battle for his survival and my own. By the last night of his life I was simply exhausted from the months of contending against the encroaching forces of destruction. Now there is an abundance of time to rest, since the fight is over. The time for striving is gone now forever.

Chapter XXXIII

Reflections on the Morning Star and the Shadows of Life

Journal entry, Avalon sunrise

Something told me to go out at early dawn and I'm glad I did. I guessed that there were just enough high clouds that a spectacular show was in store. Venus and Mars were still visible in the early light. Venus, "goddess of love," shone most brightly in the dimly lit sky. I decided to watch her, to see what would happen as the sun rose. I gazed intently, taking short breaks to observe other things occurring all around me. The clouds began to catch on fire, crimson and reddish orange, accented by deep blues and grays at the approach of the rising sun. I refocused on Venus, still as bright. Sea birds awoke. Several hundred sandpipers skittered by in the stiff, but still warm, late October breeze. Several gulls lolled by. An osprey on the hunt for breakfast sailed over the surf. A high flying jet streamed the sky with vapor trails. Increasing brightness moved in.

I began to need increasing concentration to stay glued to Venus. She began to look pale, at first imperceptibly in the ever intensifying sunlight. She began to shrink. I mused that this is how human love gets incorporated into God's love. Paradoxically, the brighter The Light shines, the lesser lights seem to diminish, even though they too are the beneficiaries of an ever brighter light. The deep blues yielded to lighter hues. A flock of terns raced seaward. Two ducks flew by. More pipers on their way to the daily dig for food. My neck began to get stiff from the long upward look. The sun, red, broke the horizon and lifted off. Venus hung on, still shining with her reflected glory. It was just a matter of time though. I stayed with her, like a man beside a deathbed, waiting for the last breath to be drawn. Some wisps of high clouds came her way, as though God in mercy for her newfound modesty would clothe her in a negligee of mist. Some floaters in my own eyes distracted my vision as I watched these strange strings of whatever float by my field of vision.

Back to Venus. She's still there, but now I must search for her anew every time I look away. She grows smaller and fainter with each passing moment. Again, I am distracted from my vigil, this time by a passing cloud. When I look again, she is gone. The sun is now blazing yellow and has assumed total dominance of the morning sky. All other lights have been subsumed in the brightness of that glory which is radiant, not reflected. This is how it will be for you and me too. We'll still be there, receiving, reflecting, but what will be central will be God's shining. God's glory will not be shared except as God gives it freely as a gift of love.

The drama seemed complete, so I turned landward to walk home. I cast a long shadow before me in the early morning sun, its light riding low, its source close to the horizon. I thought how a young man casts a long shadow toward the future, a shadow of hopes, dreams, aspirations, loves and lusts, and fears. At noon day, the days of health and maturity, no shadow is cast. We just live. We work, achieve, live, love, and hopefully learn our lessons. As we age the sun has gone before us. The shadow is now cast behind us. There is more past than future. We begin to see our leavings, our legacy, for good or for ill. We take stock, we reflect. We see how quickly it all goes by. We can't fathom how we got here so quickly. We never considered when the noonday sunshine was so bright, when its heat beat down upon us, that noon would so soon give way to evening, that twilight would come before we knew it. To paraphrase the preacher from Ecclesiastes: the sum of the matter is this: enjoy life, take pleasure in all your toil. Whatever God does endures forever. Nothing can be added nor taken away. We have eternity in our minds, but incompletely, so that we stand in awe before Thee. Amen.

Jon never got to live into the stage where the shadows stretched out behind him. He left a legacy, but did not survive into the season of reflection and wisdom. When someone dies young, this is part of the tragic dimension of their death.

Chapter XXXIV

Birthday Letter, Year III

Journal Entry, Thursday, April 10th, 2008: Letter to Jon on the occasion of his 27th birthday.

Happy birthday Jon. Of course it's probably not going to be happy down here, but I'm sure you're having a fabulous time there. I don't begrudge your happiness or your glory. I'll see you soon enough. I was remembering your birth as I was waking up this morning. We'd pleaded with you to arrive. You were ten days late. The Flyers were in the Stanley Cup play-offs, which I only mention because they're in again this year after a long time. I remember wanting to watch the game in the labor room, which convinced your mom that I was a very dopey male with no sense of real priorities. Then, as everything was fast with you, you came racing out and into the world. I just barely had time to get my gown and paper booties pulled on over my shoes, when I rushed into the delivery room and out you popped. I handed your purple, wrinkled self over to your mom, placing you at her breast, hoping that she would not be disappointed because you were a boy when she'd wanted a little girl. Of course you know there was no disappointment whatsoever. You were instantly her beloved baby boy.

I remember early mornings, bouncing you on the small exercise trampoline in our living room, with you drooling on my forearm. It's probably my fault that you never did stop bouncing through life. I remember when you hit ten pounds of weight that you needed hernia surgery, which meant no nursing on that day. So we two rose early, and I bounced with you and you drooled. Then to kill some more time and distract you from the desire to be fed, I walked you up the railroad tracks which ran behind our church. We saw a deer together. I was amazed that you did not vigorously protest the lack of breakfast with mom. Your surgery was a success and we both survived.

You started out both cute and chubby. Then you got thin and never looked back. Fortunately for me you liked your clothes extra large in your last few years. I am still wearing many of your shirts even now. They fit even though I am much heavier than you ever were because of your insistence that things be oversized. It's silly, but when I slip them on in the morning it sustains some little connection I feel with you. I guess that's why they continue to be my favorites. It's like saying, "Good morning Jon. I love you."

Anyway, I miss you greatly and love you still. Until we meet again, Love, Dad.

Chapter XXXV

The First Year Is Not the Hardest

I blush to think of how often before Jon's death I told a bereaved person that the first year would be the hardest. They would face all the holidays, birthdays, anniversaries and other special occasions for the first time without their loved one on hand. This gives the illusion of being wise counsel but it is not for several reasons.

For one thing, it is not unusual to spend many months simply numb. Severe grief often results in a pervasive emotional and spiritual pallor. The color and delight of living simply drains away into the shadows of sadness. Next Monday is as likely to bring a surprise lightning bolt of grief as is a birthday next month or an anniversary three months away. I remember way back in my time in Arkansas when I was but 21 years old, walking on a grassy lane on our farm when suddenly out of nowhere two F15 fighter planes roared overhead not high above the treetops. They certainly grabbed my attention! Grief often comes like a stealth fighter, unannounced and we are not prepared for its arrival. It does not check with our planning or with our expectations. Grief's estimated time of arrival, its ETA is unknown.

Near the end of our third grieving year, I was conducting a wedding at a large local ballroom. The wedding service was conducted, the hour for refreshments concluded, and we were summoned to our seats for dinner. The DJ began to play a selection of music.

Just months before Jon died, in the late night hours of his addiction, he made CD's of selected music and gave them to family and friends. After he died, the lyrics to the music he chose were like windows into his heart. Jean and I rarely could listen without weeping. Sure enough, on came the rendition with a Jamaican feel of "Somewhere Over the Rainbow/What a Wonderful World." This sent Jean to the ladies room in tears. I could not get to her, so I sat and waited. She returned, unsure as to whether or not she was going to be able to handle the situation.

Just when we both thought we could pull ourselves together, another tune from Jon's CD came on which was the final strike. We looked at each other and knew our evening there was over. We took our leave and headed home. Fortunately, the family understood our heart condition to sufficient degree and they were gracious. The stealth fighter of grief had landed another surgical strike with uncanny accuracy.

I recall another instance, probably in the second year or early in the third. I was driving to a committee meeting of our presbytery one evening, and was stopped at a light about fifteen miles from home. I looked to my left and there was a motorcycle shop that I had visited with Jon, where he helped me pick out my first helmet and riding gloves. I was stabbed with sorrow and tears began to run.

Jon had wanted a motorcycle and I had resolutely said no, not while you live with me. I don't want to have to care for a quadriplegic. The day he arrived home with his super hot sport bike, he was proud, and I was angry. It felt to me like an in-your-face act of disrespect. In time, I relented and came to see the bike as an expression of Jon's passion for adventure. It was also another unaffordable toy which eventually came fully equipped with hounding creditors.

I began to teach a group of men at church from the book and course, Wild at Heart, by John Eldridge. This material was great at bringing men's hearts alive and re-igniting their passion. Jon and his friend Brad attended and seemed to enjoy the group. I was looking for a way to connect more deeply with my son as I fought for his survival. The truth is, I had always wanted a motorcycle myself but had never pursued it. Jon began to dream with me that I would at last get my own bike and we would ride together. I went to the state run, safe rider's course up in Sea Girt, New Jersey, took the test, and got my motorcycle operator's license.

I took Jon's hot wheels out for some rides. Most people thought I was having a mid-life crisis, or that I had lost all sense. The latter may have been true; the former was inaccurate, since I'd already had my mid-life transition years before. Jon took me shopping for a bike of my own. Just as I was about to take the leap and purchase my own bike, I awoke one night and came to my senses. Jon's debt on our credit cards was already far too high. He had charmed and cajoled us into a deep financial hole that would already take us years from which to extricate ourselves. I had no business adding bike payments on top of this burden.

Shortly thereafter, Jon's own financial house of cards began to come apart at the seams. A young man bought Jon's bike, and one set of creditors was finally off of our phone and off of our backs. Still it was a sad day. It felt like dreams were dying all around us. Jon was not making his truck payments, so a friend who is a car dealer bought him out and sold him a small Dodge for transportation until Jon could get back on his feet. All of this was horrible for Jon to endure. He loved his truck; he hated that car. It represented defeat.

All of these painful, bittersweet memories flooded my mind in an instant before the light turned green. I drove on through my tears to do my ministerial duty, but my heart was not in it.

The work of grief takes way longer than most people expect. A year is not really very long. Those who have never faced hard grief may not have a clue at all that is involved for a person on this path. What I mean by hard grief is grief that is either caused by the death of someone who was very close, a lifelong mate perhaps, or the death resulting from tragic circumstances.

My grief was of a far different order when my ailing aunt Fran who was 95 finally got her wish to go on into eternity than when my dear son died at age 24. She was close and I loved her dearly but her advanced age and deteriorating health emptied losing her of the tragic dimension of loss. Her death issued in a measure of celebration made possible because of our shared belief in Christ and his promise of eternal life. Fran's death did not produce the shock waves that Jon's death created in full measure. Hers was a triumphant home going after a long and faithful life. His felt like a too early snatching away of precious gifts and promises.

Further, the literature on the subject of death and dying can be at once helpful and misleading. It is helpful to see described some of the emotions that you will experience as you grieve, because there come times when you wonder if what you are feeling is "normal." It helps some to hear that others have felt similar emotions and experienced like difficulties to the ones you are going through. The experience of grief due to the death of a child can be so intense you feel like you may be losing your mind. You wonder if you will ever be able to get back from the far country of your sorrow.

It has become popular to talk about the stages of dying and grieving from denial, to bargaining, to anger, to acceptance, all of which are certainly parts of the experience of grieving and it is helpful to be able to recognize them as component parts of the process. But they do not march across our emotional and spiritual landscape like a parade with characters appearing in a neat succession. They appear more in the manner that a friend used to describe his four year old soccer team; they are like sixteen kids who swarm around the ball like ants on fruit.

It is normal to bounce around from one stage to another. I may be angry one moment, accepting the next, and in denial the next, back to anger, and so on and on. Perhaps the word stage is itself misleading. To go in stages implies something like ascending a staircase, rising one step after another until the top is reached. Grieving in my experience is much more chaotic and disjointed than that. It seems far from being sequential at the time one is enduring it.

One of the least helpful concepts foisted on people in sorrow is that of closure. "I hope you can achieve closure." What is that supposed to mean? If love is strong, there is no such thing, nor is closure a sought-after outcome. What we want is to discover new ways to hold the beloved in our hearts, to hold our hearts open in their direction with love that has not been extinguished. The goal is not to put them or our relationship in some storage vault of the past, close and lock the door, and move on with our lives. The goal is rather to find a creative way to carry them forward in our hearts until we meet again in eternity. If what people mean by closure is that grief changes in nature over time and one learns to live peaceably with the presence of the absence, then yes, I'll cede the point.

Writing as I am now nearly four years after Jon's death I can say that the grief does lose some of its intensity and its ability to dominate every waking hour. I now have whole days where I am not sad, and the sadness I do experience is not debilitating. Sadness visits me often, but the level of intensity has finally diminished. The sorrow now functions often as a teacher, as a compass needle that directs me to gold. But this certainly was not the case in the first year.

My experience has been that the third year was somehow harder than the first or the second year. Perhaps the sabbatical provided some distraction from the task during the second year. I've pondered why the third year was so hard. I began to experience a feeling of a growing weight of the finality of Jon's absence. He was not coming back, not ever. Which I knew of course, but maybe I didn't know it in some deep recesses of my own soul. It finally dawned upon me that I would not one day awaken from the bad dream of child loss. I was already awake and this was my new reality. I will always be a father who has lost a son. There is no going back. That fact will never change.

Jean also began to have more intensified sad days, days when she had the blues, days when she missed her baby boy. Jon was her soul mate, her companion, her responsibility, and her friend. I think the finality of his absence began to weigh more heavily upon her as well. There remains a symbiotic relationship between her sorrow and mine; when she's sad, I'm sad, not just for my loss but for hers also.

Chapter XXXVI

Prayers for Year III

Father, I would have never guessed how hard this grief would be after two years of what seemed like hard sorrowing. I guess the finality of Jon's absence has finally sunk down deep into my soul. I need you now more than ever to comfort me in this affliction. And you have been comforting and have been so faithful. Lord, you know that I am no longer angry or even disappointed with you. That burden has passed. I am deeply convinced that you are nothing but good and you mean nothing but good for me and all whom I love and for whom I care. I feel it in my work when I pray for people. I am relaxed and confident in you. I no longer beg and plead. I simply make my requests and trust you to do the best. So, do the best for me and for Jean now, as you see fit. I wait upon you. With love, your son, Bill. Amen

O Lord, you know when I sit and when I rise, when I go out and when I come in. You know my sins, my faults, my shortcomings, my omissions as well as my commissions. Forgive me and cleanse me from unrighteous deeds, from unholy attitudes and from "stinking thinking." I am so limited in understanding. I humble myself before your perfect will and plan. Deliver me from false paths to false comforts that lead to dead ends filled with dead things. Have mercy upon me, for I am brought low in sorrow. Lift up my head that I may joyfully praise you once more. Through Jesus Christ our Lord, Amen.

How long O Lord, how long? This anguish seems like a fire that will not be extinguished. When I control it in one place, it bursts into flame somewhere else. Lord, I need your help to persevere through what seems like an endless forced march down a trail of tears. My heart is parched and dry on too many days. Other days, I begin to feel I might have a renewed joy in living. I'm clinging to you in your faithfulness and your love. Thank you for the constancy that you have shown me through this awful time. Forgive my speech with you which at times has arisen, harsh and arrogant, out of the pit of my sorrows. I am comforted to know that you are well acquainted with our grief; in fact you have born our grief and carried our sorrows, surely! Have mercy upon me Lord and do not hold the sins of my soul against me. In your tender compassion, cleanse me from guilt, and accept me your wounded child. For the sake of your name, and for my own sake, I pray to you Lord Jesus. Amen.

Chapter XXXVII

Third Birthday AD

Journal entry, April 25th, 2008: Avalon. When Jean and I were young, the ocean, the beach, made her exuberant like a little girl. Now the empty, wide open expanse, the wind, waves, and sand only bring her too many thoughts of Jon and his absence. We used to walk together there, and laugh, and love. Now I walk alone with my own thoughts. I explore, beach comb, pick up little ocean artifacts, still with interest, but with no one to show and no one with whom to share them. This is but one of the myriad of ways that life is now so different since Jon died.

Journal Entry, July 23rd, 2008: The third anniversary of Jon's death.
6:20 AM. The fateful day. I awoke for the rerun memory film on cue at 2:30 AM, but declined the invitation to watch the mental replay of the night Jon died. I had a counseling session last evening where the suffering skills came into play as they now often do. I'm still gold mining. We've no plans for today, so I don't know how we'll spend it.

Dear Jon,
Today it's been three years. I trust you are doing well in eternity. Life down here continues to be tough. We all miss you very much. I've started writing that book I've been threatening,

but it's tough and slow going. My grief over you continues to change. I am able now to remember more and more of the good things as some of the addiction horrors take their place and are balanced by other happy memories.

Mom continues to carry a very broken heart and she so misses you and your kindred heart. She seems very alone and unreachable in vast regions of her soul. I too feel often comfortless. Not too many people want to hear about it after three years. I suppose we should seek and try a support group, but I doubt we will.

So how is heaven anyway? I'm increasingly aware of myself growing older, with limitations setting in. I still have trouble letting go of the sentiment that you were the one appointed to be our old age helper. Glad you escaped that one! Who knows, maybe I won't even have an old age. I'm trying to shed the illusion of control and self determination. Your death certainly gave me a hearty dose of reality on that score. I want you to know that I still love you deeply. I think my anger is almost totally gone, but who knows what residual stuff lies in the soul's basement somewhere? But, day to day, I recall you with mostly a sense of great loss.

Mom ran into Ben, your old boss at the pharmacy, at the Shop Rite recently and he broke down and cried with her right there on the spot. You touched a lot of people in your short life. I can't wait to see you with a perfected heart (I can't wait to see myself in that condition either), beyond the reach of both our sin and our addictions, and all tears and sorrow. Until then my young, now ancient, eternal son, much love from this place to your place, Dad.

Chapter XXXVIII

Scary Prayer

Journal entry, August 2ⁿᵈ, 2008

Paige's doctor was still concerned about her knee and this one really guts me! (Paige is my first granddaughter and "The" princess; she was diagnosed with Osgood's slaughter and small stress fractures running vertically up her femur, a potentially serious condition which required her to go some months with no-impact activities and possibly to face surgery in the future.) *I had some rather frightening reactions toward the Lord, which I even hesitate to report. My first was, "Don't you dare let this happen!" This is not a very good way to talk to almighty God. Talk about presumption and foolishness! My second reaction was to think, "Do not bother to pray," because, (a) God doesn't answer my prayers, or, (b) I don't want to face another disappointment and the resultant struggle with doubt. Forgive me please Lord on all counts. I have no excuse. I'm living frightened I guess since Jon's death, and angry, and disappointed, and shaken, and beaten into fatalism. I don't know what. To whom shall I go Lord? You have the words of eternal life. Please, please, heal Paige and have mercy upon her and me too. I choose again this day to trust in you, in the midst of this fallen place, to trust you.*

Journal entry, September 4th, 2008

Thanks Lord for the good word of healing in Paige's leg. I confess I've had evil and frightening thoughts about what my already weakened faith would endure had she not been well. My deep sense of vulnerability to everything is a hard place to find peace. I wonder how much of what I am experiencing is related to Jon's death. Are there time bombs with delayed fuses lying around in my soul which detonate without warning and blow up suddenly causing me trouble? In any event, I need daily forgiveness and more forbearance than any person has a right to request, let alone expect. I'm holding on for dear life. Have mercy, Lord, have mercy. If you don't, I'm lost.

Journal entry, September 5th, 2008

I'm sorry and ashamed of my heart attitudes toward you Lord. Jean struggles too. She's enveloped in a relentless sadness. I wish I could help her, and us both. But I can't. I just keep on trying to serve and hope we'll come out of this someday.

Chapter XIX

Teaching

During the period just after Jon died when I was reading everything I could about death and dying and grief, one of the best little books I read was, <u>Don't Sing Songs to a Heavy Heart</u>, by Robert Haugk. The title is taken from Proverbs 25:20, "Like one who takes away a garment on a cold day, or like vinegar poured on soda, is one who sings songs to a heavy heart." A note on the cover says, "The words and actions we use in our attempts to help hurting people may unintentionally add to their burdens instead of easing their pain." Dr. Hauck is the founder of Stephen Ministries which trains lay people to be skilled care givers. The book is packed with practical dos and don'ts for those who would help and not hurt a hurting or grieving person. I determined that when I felt ready I would teach the contents of this book to a group within my congregation. This I did during the third year.

Once again, the process of transforming sorrow into positive ministry was a form of discovering gold. I spoke openly in the class about my experience of being ministered to during my bereavement. I have first hand knowledge of what helps, what doesn't, and what hurts. My people loved the study and were most attentive and diligent, in some degree more than usual because I, the leader, had been through such an awful time.

This was no longer an academic exercise for me or for them. I could see many of them joining with me in the painful process of facing up to all the ways we had mishandled the sorrows of people in our lives. They learned and became wiser for the next time that they would encounter someone with a broken heart. And I received a measure of healing for having led them through the study.

Journal entry: November 29th, 2008. Jean's birthday.

Since Jon died it seems like I've been in a slow, relentless process of being stripped. All righteousness except Jesus' righteousness removed. Me, the things I don't want to do, I do, the good I will, I don't. Wretched man that I am; who will deliver me? Usefulness? Diminished. Expertise? Suspect. Health? Threatened. Prowess? Drying up. Illusions of youth? Prayer? Belief? All coming under the shadow of death. I rarely ask the Lord for concrete answers for situations. Is this resignation? Despair? Unbelief? I give thanks and ask for mercy for the impoverished condition of my soul. I eat, work, play, love, sleep as best I can. I try to take pleasure in my toil. Beyond these things I no longer harbor grandiose visions of being "super preacher" changing the world. I'm just being with people. I'm not taking them anywhere. If a leader is someone who has followers, what is someone sitting in the middle of a group like a flightless duck in a winter pond. A dead duck or an albatross? So this morning, the eve of the first Sunday of Advent, I must craft a sermon on Jesus' final coming. Great! Another opportunity for the Holy Spirit to rescue me! (At this point, a sign was given: my pen ran out of ink. Shut up Bill!)

One day, early in the fourth year after Jon died, I spoke with my dear friend and Jon's counselor Austin. He asked me if I had read The Shack, by William Paul Young. I said no, I'd never heard of it before. He recommended it. Jean and I returned from several days in Avalon to find that Al and Nancy, our friends from New Hampshire, had mailed us a copy. We soon discovered that the book was causing quite a stir around the nation and even around the world. Some loved it, some didn't.

The story line involves the central character Mack, whose youngest daughter was abducted and murdered while he and his children were on a camping trip. Young tells a remarkable tale from that point of departure, a work of what I would call non-fiction fiction. It is a novel, a made up story, with beautiful truth conveyed. What I found extremely helpful was the title that Mack bestowed upon his grief; he named it The Great Sadness. From the moment I read it, I was immensely helped. This *thing* has a name!

Like Mack, this fictional but oh so real character, I too had been wearing my sorrow like a mantel or a shroud. I was learning to live with it, to carry it around. I lost sight of what life might be like without its constant lurking presence. I was a father who had lost a son. My loss began to shape my identity and take me over. When I would preach words of life and hope, deep inside, the Great Sadness would accuse me of hypocrisy, or of unfaithfulness. Notions that life could once again be joyous and full even without Jon were like acts of adultery. I was married to the Great Sadness and the covenant should not be violated.

The act of naming what was heretofore un-named was like instant liberation. Naming the Great Sadness was like seeing the Wizard of Oz behind the shroud. The Great Sadness had become the Great Pretender, claiming far more of me than was right. In the light of day, I got a huge chunk of my soul back. The name of the Great Sadness had to be brought captive and made to submit to the name that is above every name, the name of Jesus.

Chapter XL

The Alchemy of
Sharing Life in the Pit

"You've brought me here, where things are clear
And trials turn to gold."

Keith Green

My encounter with Mary Ann six months after Jon died, as we met in my study to talk and pray over the death of her son and mine was a foretaste of things to come. I discovered then, and have continued to experience since, how the power of the Holy Spirit flows most poignantly through our sorrows. The deeper the sorrow, the deeper the comfort. In sharing what she feared would hurt me, she helped to break the sense of isolation I was feeling. Here was another human being with a sorrow commensurate with my own. This interchange of two people in the pit of sorrow served not to increase the pain, but rather to deepen the comfort. This dynamic has played out over and over in the months and years since.

Being a pastor, perhaps I have a leg up on other people in my situation. It is a privileged and most times honored position. People invite me into the sacred places of their sufferings and their sorrows. I have the sense of standing on holy ground. Who am I after all to be so trusted with such intimate access to the things so close to the inner life of people and their families?

I am invited into the times of joy and celebration, the anniversaries, the weddings, the baptisms, the graduations. I am also included in the times of deepest sorrow. A divorce is demanded. A child is still born. A person suddenly is diagnosed with cancer. A young father dies leaving a wife and children to fend for themselves. A child tragically dies. The call comes. I go. I offer presence, compassion, I offer Christ. Answers? No. Solutions? Occasionally. What takes place is a privilege and a mystery. People are helped. People are comforted. It is not because of me. I am a participant in something bigger than them and me put together in the crucible of life.

Chapter XLI

Changes

After Jon died, I became a different person, and a different pastor. The first thing that dawned upon me was how many people I had failed. I was not working at a sufficient depth. The quality of my pastoral care was severely lacking. I had to let this painful insight confront me and take effect. The process was humbling, or should I say humiliating. It's not that I intended to do shoddy work; I just did my work at a more shallow level than I have since the suffering of this grief served as my teacher. That insight was also like finding gold.

I noticed that my relationship with my congregation had subtly changed. The level of trust and appreciation had gone up. They became more attentive to my preaching. My words carried more weight. They knew I would not traffic in superficial religious bromides for the vicissitudes of life. My pain and sorrow made me more authentic. My suffering added depth to my work.

Some of the questions of doubt and despair have undergone a transformation as well. Out of my damaged trust arose the question, "If this can happen, what else can happen?" This has changed subtly to, "After going through this, why should I worry about that?" I am now free of obsessing over things which I have no ability to control. This freedom has many tangible results for me both in ministry and in my personal life.

For instance, my congregation is, on paper, nearly three hundred members, with an annual budget of $300,000. In actuality, there are one hundred and fifty members shouldering the load in terms of participation and financial support. Late in November of 2007, we were over $100,000 in the red. I went to the Lord in prayer and was questioned by the Spirit: "Is there anything you can do about this that you have not already tried? This is not your problem. If I want the church to close, you won't be able to keep it open. If I want the church to stay open, you won't be able to close it. Rest in my provision and trust me." We have indeed survived and I look forward to discovering the ways that God will provide for us to do God's work. God is restoring my capacity to trust him. With renewed trust comes renewed freedom and peace.

In my pastor's prayer group, I am the lone Presbyterian among Methodists. Since I was baptized by a Methodist bishop and raised in the Methodist church, I guess you could say I've reconnected with my root system. These men have been my listening hearts as I've walked this excruciating path. We meet once a week for several hours to talk shop, share the concerns of our lives in general, and to pray. Underlying our time lays the Wesleyan question, "How is it with your soul." After so many months of reporting to them the shape of my sorrow filled soul, finally, in this the fourth year after Jon died, I am now reporting to them, much to the relief of their long-suffering ears, new levels of peace and of a returning joy.

One of the things that has happened over time is the rebalancing of memories. During the last several years of Jon's life, the dominant issues in our relationship centered on the problems caused by his addiction. I was angry most of the time. I was angry because of the lying. I was angry because of the betrayals. I was angry because of the disrespect I felt toward me, and even angrier at the disrespect I saw toward Jean. I was angry because Jon played Jean like a fiddle and often was able to pit her against me, and sometimes me against her. I understood how a child could drive a wedge between two parents to get what they want because I myself had been a past master of this manipulative art in my own youthful rebellion. I was furious to see it being applied to me. I was deeply wounded, over and over again, as we danced to the addict's tune of recovery followed by relapse. 'Round and 'round, she goes, and where she stops, nobody knows. I was enraged at the whole drug scene as I watched my son and my whole family being gutted and filleted under its influence.

Jean and I prayed, cried, begged and pleaded with both Jon and God, fought in any way we could, spent tons of money, and searched far and wide for help. Underneath the anger lurked the fear, which haunted our nights, robbing us of sleep, and stalked us by day, leaving us no peace. There was my beloved son, and then there was my son on drugs. They were two different people locked up in one body. Life had become torture. These were the dominant feelings I had at the time of Jon's death, the ones that all the advice books urged me to be sure to share. My "son on drugs" had pretty much devoured "my son not on drugs" in my emotional world. This was an unbalanced distortion that needed to be redressed, and I have found that over these nearly four years, a new balance has been emerging as I allow the good memories of Jon to take their rightful place in my recollection and in my heart.

Journal entry: January 6ᵗʰ, 2009

The grief is still around, though I haven't written much about it lately. It pays me visits but I would have to say that it is no longer such a dominant presence in my life. Its edges are blunter. I have many waking hours where it's not on my mind. I have a renewed sense of the wonder of life, the goodness of God, and I trust in the Lord. Once in a while a doubt bird flies by with jabs like, "What if the whole thing, eternal life and all those things you say you believe are not true, are just a fairy tale, etc. etc.", but I refuse to let them nest in my hair! I've returned to the original plan to scatter Jon's ashes in the ocean, after a brief time considering a conventional burial. Both Mark and Julia were not at all receptive to the idea of placing Jon's ashes in the ground. There is a part of me that would like to scatter them by myself in solitude, but I must not exclude Jean and the kids. I have no right to be so selfish.

I shared that desire to scatter Jon's ashes by myself in my prayer group this morning and Larry questioned me about it with some incredulity. It gave me pause. I guess I envision the experience as being nothing for both Jean and Julia but a gut wrenching episode tearing open the wounds all over again. And I guess it's hard for me to see them grieving and not assume some responsibility to comfort them. Solitude is much less complicated. Mark could do it with me I think and probably have a similar emotional response. I guess it's still too soon to know what to do and with whom to do it, and besides the decision is not mine to make on my own. Still with the permission of all involved, I would take care of casting Jon's earthly remains to the sea. (May 12th, 2009)

Chapter XLII

Fourth Birthday AD

Good Friday, April 10th, 2009. 7:30 AM. Journal Entry.

Dear Jon,

Happy Birthday. You'd have been 28 today. I guess you are timeless there. We all still miss you terribly. I was walking in the park with Paige, Logan, and Jonny G. yesterday and told them it would be your birthday today. We had quite a talk about death and heaven, where were you buried, where were we to scatter your ashes and so on. We all look forward to seeing you again. Logan (age 5) said he was in a hurry to die and go to heaven because he loves to swim and he was sure God would give him a big pool. We all said how we love Jesus. I wonder what it is like in glory. Julia is still running from her grief over your departure. Mom is apprehensive about this day. Sorrow still ambushes us all I guess. I'm not sure where Mark is with it all. We don't talk nearly often enough. I must correct that somehow. Jonny G. has taken great delight in discovering and pilfering treasures from your old toy box. I'm still wearing your shirts most days and think of you every time I put one on. It has become sort of a comforting ritual for me.

As you know, I'm trying to write a book about grief. It's slow going. Mom and I are going to Avalon next week and I hope to get more written, I've been undisciplined and consciously avoiding putting pressure on myself in the effort, but maybe it is time to add some pressure to the mix lest I never get it done. I fear that some of my ideas have already escaped into forgetfulness. I hope that the Holy Spirit will bring back the good stuff. Well my dear one, the coffee's done and I'm rambling on. I have the three hour Good Friday service later today. I'm preaching on the 7th of the last words of Christ on the cross; "Into thy hands I commit my spirit." Into His hands I have committed your spirit and mine too, in full trust and faith on behalf of both of us. Have a heavenly blast. I'll see you soon.

With deep love, Dad.

Chapter XLIII

Real Presence

Her friend called and asked if I would see her. She had lost her husband to pancreatic cancer six months before. Her oldest son had been incarcerated due to his heroin addiction. Her youngest son was living at home, a raging alcoholic. She needed someone to talk to. We made an appointment for them to come in. Friends and neighbors were helping her and advising her, with increasing frustration, because no matter how good their advice concerning how to deal with her alcoholic son, she would agree but refuse to act. "You are enabling him. You need to exercise tough love. Tell him to shape up or move out. Don't encourage his drinking by being codependent. Next time he gets in trouble refuse to bail him out. Stop rescuing him."

I'd heard it all before, over and over. I said it myself, to myself, and to Jean. I was painfully acquainted with both the well-intended and frustrated advisors who seek to come to our aid, and with the emotionally paralyzed heart condition of this mother, now a widow in the throes of a very young grief. She was like kin to me. She was barely beginning to emerge from the numb state of early grief, and was facing immense losses through the lives of both of her sons.

Once again, I found myself tapping into the seam of gold lying deep in the pit of my own history of sorrow. I listened without trying to fix her, because I now know the impossibility of one human being trying to fix another. None of us are problems for other people to solve. We are living breathing human beings who operate out of the center of our hearts if we but will. Many among us are cut off from contact with our own hearts because they have been so wounded and abused in the course of living that we have set up a wall of defense against our very own being, not to mention the beneficent attempts of others to come close.

So often in pastoral counseling I gently urge people to trust their heart, especially if Christ dwells there by faith. We get confused at this point spiritually because the Bible describes the heart as being desperately wicked and therefore impossible to understand. But when a person comes to Christ by faith and His living presence enters the human heart by the agency and working of the Holy Spirit, they now have a new governor in the very core of their being that operates in all the wisdom and goodness of our creator and redeemer. This is the heart that can be trusted if we can but learn to connect with it.

The heart devoid of that presence of the Lord is untrustworthy to be sure. In great sorrow or in times of affliction, we can become so damaged that we temporarily lose the ability to discern and trust what our hearts are telling us. Our prayers, a main avenue for sustaining that connection may grow stale and cold and we find ourselves cut off from our comforter. True prayer is built upon real trust, and often trials hurt our ability to trust.

Advice appeals to our intellect and is mostly ineffective in its attempt to bypass the heart and its reasons. It may in fact be both true and wise counsel, but so often we are conflicted to the point of being unable to act upon what is offered. It sounds good. We believe the testimonies of how similar advice may have "worked" for others, but unless we can accept it through our own hearts, it will not help us. The appeal to our minds and wills that excludes the priorities of the heart is doomed to fall ineffective in the dust.

We spent an hour together, this severely bruised woman and her friend and me. She was comforted and her isolation was diminished, if only for just a moment. I felt as she left that she had a sense of having received the gift of understanding and a certain peace enveloped her being. She exuded great gratitude for the time and the listening which validated her without trying to change her to suit some predetermined template for "handling" her son and her situation. I also very gently tried to set her friend free of wearing the fixer's mantle as she sought to help her friend. Whether or not she heard me I'm not sure.

Chapter XLIV

Missing You

April 30th, 2009

Dear Jon,

I'm sitting in my study and I just was rereading some of <u>The Shack</u>, preparing to lead Sunday night's discussion group. Mack, in his visionary experience, has just buried the remains of his slain daughter, Missy. Papa, the figure for God the Father, "came up next to him and put his arm over his shoulder. 'Missy is incredible; you know that. Truly, she loves you.'" "I miss her terribly...it still hurts so much," was Mack's response.

Reading this, I found my self weeping and missing you terribly too and still hurting, so I just felt to write you a note this morning. I think I'm beginning to get some new ideas for ministry I must do in our family to move our healing along. After all this time we still all have much unfinished business to do with our sorrows. I'll let you know how it goes. Much love from earth, Dad.

Chapter XLV

Prayers for Year IV

Dear Father, I can praise you now from a heart that has received against all the resistance of sorrow the comfort of your love. I have begun to emerge from what feels like a forty year sojourn in the wilderness of bitter questioning and feelings of isolation. I know now that you have always been with me even in the times that in the anger of my hurt I have treated you as an unwelcome guest whom I could no longer trust. I was never more wrong in all my life and I thank you for understanding that the bitter gall would one day ebb away and be replaced again by a loving confidence in your goodness. Thank you for looking beyond my momentary rancor and bitterness and for delivering me into a renewed faith in you. With love and gratitude through Jesus, Amen.

Lord Jesus, I have come into a season now in which I am looking through the eyes of faith and seeing your beauty and your sweetness with fresh vision. My life from day to day has become an adventure of learning to minister to your Presence in my life, my work, and my world. I am finally experiencing long stretches of peace; a peace that only months ago was not even hoped for, let alone expected to come. Your visitation through the Holy Spirit which has come as an abiding presence fills me with comfort and strength. I still have many times of sadness that come upon me, but I meet them with the sense that you are holding me up in the confrontation with my great loss. I still miss my son so very much and still am moved to tears. In fact, it's as though my emotions have been rejuvenated, being lifted out of the deep freeze of my grief. I am more alive now even in my sadness. It is good to feel the full range of emotions, even when they are wild and unmanageable. Thank you Lord for being with me, my constant friend and lover of my soul. Amen.

Lord, four years have somehow gone by when time seemed to stand still. The work of grief has been agonizingly slow. My awareness of your unhurried presence has been steadily growing. I look back now embarrassed by the months and months that I felt lost in your absence. I see now that you never were far from me. It was all too easy for me to be consumed by my fears and my sorrows. I may have finally learned a degree of courage that I have never known before. I pray that my new confidence may always be harnessed in service for you and never become the servant of my presumption. Amen.

Lord Jesus, You have patiently taught me to mine for gold in the pit of sorrow. The rich ore of your love is repeatedly to be found right in the midst of my wounds. I have been given great gifts of sensitivity in the practice of ministry to my fellow bereaved sufferers. In the meeting of our hearts there flows a sweet comfort back and forth between us. I receive comfort as you employ me to give it. It is the economy of heaven. I know that you collect our tears in your bottle and you do not waste one iota of our sorrows. I consecrate myself to you. The privilege of serving you has become once again the joy of my life. Thank you so much. Amen

Chapter XLVI

Gold Mining

"If there is no eternal consciousness in a human being, if at the bottom of everything there is only a wild ferment, a power that, twisting in dark passions, produces everything great or inconsequential; if an unfathomable, insatiable emptiness lies hidden beneath everything, what would life be then but despair? If this is the way life is, if there is no sacred bond uniting mankind, if one generation rises up after another like the leaves of the forest, if one generation succeeds the other as the songs of birds in the woods, if the human race passes through the world as a ship through the sea or the wind through the desert, a thoughtless and fruitless whim, if an eternal oblivion always lurks hungrily for its prey and there is no power strong enough to wrest it from its clutches-how empty and devoid of consolation life would be!" Soren Kierkegaard. [6]

In the literature of spiritual direction, there is the recognition of two movements of the Spirit as Christ is formed in people, that of desolation and that of consolation. As the faces of the void menace us with death and dying, disease and decay, relational disintegration and all other sorts of afflictions, we need to know that there is an eternal yes and an eternal no. God says an emphatic "No!" to all that would ultimately destroy his children. The eternal yes of God literally speaks life into the void, emptying death and all its lesser expressions of their ultimate power. The penultimate word is death. The last word is life!

As soon as I began to get a glimpse of the gold to be mined in the pit of sorrow, I determined that I would go get it. I would go as deeply as I must and as deeply as I could. To shrink away in cowardice would be to consign Jon's death to the dominion of despair. It would be to succumb to the notion that his life was an isolated bead on a necklace with no real significance beyond himself. Kierkegaard describes the emptiness of this view so very well. This I was not and am not willing to do.

My faith and the inner witness of the Spirit tells me that life and love and the inter-relatedness of all beings are stronger than the hatred and alienation and death that surround us and seek to convince us that they are the ultimate fate of all, no matter how hard we resist. The resurrection of Jesus of Nazareth is the ultimate cosmic shout of victory over the principalities and powers and spiritual hosts of wickedness in the heavenly places. And the judgment upon death itself is rendered: death is a vain pretender when confronted by the power of Almighty God.

Somewhere along the way, whoever we are and whomever we have lost, no matter what we have suffered, the questions of our hearts must be laid aside and a decision must be made. It all comes down to a choice in the end. The questions to be decided are: Whom do you trust? What will you believe? How much will you risk for your decision? Will you bet all of your heart upon what you have decided? To hedge your bets, to play it cool, to live devoid of passion is a dead end leading to mediocrity and just plain boredom with life, or worse, it is to consign ourselves to life long bondage to the fear of death.. We were made for something far more engaging and enduring than this.

Our consolation arises from the faith that dares to believe, as Kierkegaard was fond of saying, in virtue of the absurd. The pain in our hearts, the losses, disappointments and betrayals push us in the direction of mistrust, cynicism, unbelief, and despair. But the Holy Spirit invades our souls with a different set of experiences, inspirations, revelations, and insights into the true nature of our lives. We are invited to acknowledge the goodness and kindness of our God. We are summoned to taste and see that the Lord is good and that His steadfast love endures for ever. Sorrow may endure for a night, but joy comes in the morning.

Chapter XLVII

Facing New Fears

Here in the fourth year, I've been tracking an emergent anxiety, a face of the void that I resisted seeing for some time. It has forced its way into the light in spite of all my efforts to avoid it. Jon's death has forced me to look at the prospects of further losses just up ahead. Perhaps it is because at this juncture I am just days away now from my sixtieth birthday, and wondering how in the world this has happened to a man who even still feels like a youth inside. I'm not old yet, but I can feel the encroachments of age accumulating in my life.

People say that it is the hardest thing in the world to lose a child. I have had to finally admit that I'm not so sure. The hardest loss I can imagine and the one that has emerged for me as a real terror is the thought that I one day could lose Jean. I guess I had a foretaste of this during the period of grief where Jean and I were so emotionally divided in our own private sorrows.

We have had a running, somewhat frivolous banter going for several years about who will go first, each of us flippantly vying for the honor of preceding the other in making our grand exit. Our ideal is to both go out together, but what are the odds of that happening? She accuses me of having a morbid sense of humor, but it may be that I am, and we are together, engaged in whistling past the graveyard.

Jean and I met at sixteen. We have been best and lifelong friends. We have known many joys as well as endured many trials and sorrows together. We have been faithful to each other throughout our marriage. We have sought and received great blessings and much healing in the depth of our hearts from the Lord. These are all grand and glorious things and the list could be greatly expanded, but the haunting part of the fear that stalks me now is the thought of losing the myriad of little intimacies and idiosyncrasies that we notice and share in everyday life. The unique things that amuse me about her, even the occasional things that annoy me, would all rise up to haunt me were they to be snatched away in death. Morning coffee and afternoon tea, happy hours and dinner hours, the silence of long car rides together when very few words are spoken, not because we have nothing to say, but because our silence is itself a form of communication, these are the threads that entwine our lives in a deeply satisfying shared intimacy. We are both delighted and secure in each others' presence. I would miss her charming dyslexic gaffes and reversals of numbers, words, and thoughts. I would be intensely lonely at meal times, free times, and bedtimes, and just about every time. "Alone" is the menacing face of the void! It is a face I learned to recognize all too well when Jon died.

In what is now over thirty years of ministry, I have conducted hundreds of funerals for people of all ages, and have ministered to so many newly bereft widowers and widows. Some of the deaths were a relief, ending long sieges of suffering of one sort or another, some have come shockingly and suddenly, some have come at ripe old age and others have come at tragically young ages, leaving a mate and often young children behind to try to pick up the pieces of a shattered family.

I have read the scriptures, prayed the prayers, offered eulogies and meditations, and tried to faithfully proclaim the hope of the resurrection and to lift up the name of Jesus in each situation as the Spirit gave me utterance. I have stood by many a grave and said the words of committal and prayed that we the living would go forth to serve the Lord with whatever days remain left to each of us, "knowing that in the Lord our labors are not in vain." I have seen numerous American flags tightly folded into the prescribed triangle and handed to a surviving mate by a military color guard. I have heard the bagpipes drone "Amazing Grace" and watched families and friends place one last flower on the lid of the casket before it is lowered out of sight in the bowels of the earth.

In all the years up until Jon died, in numerous cemeteries and under widely divergent circumstances which brought me there, I never used the ancient liturgical phrase, "earth to earth, ashes to ashes, dust to dust, in the sure and certain hope of the resurrection." I seem to recall a seminary professor advising against using the phrase, deeming it too depressing. Since Jon's death though, I have been using it. I have come to see the power to comfort in the stark directness of these simple words. In them we proclaim the power of God to work life out of our most inert elements, earth, ashes, and dust. Our creation story names these as our point of origin. We say without apology and without so much as a blush, that our God is able to accomplish the resurrection of the body in spite of the ravages of death. The phrase is a muscular declaration and is full of the courage of faith. "Earth to earth, ashes to ashes, dust to dust, in sure and certain hope of the resurrection." We commit her body to the ground. We commend him to your eternal care. The old liturgies of the Church serve us so well.

I came across a prayer of Kierkegaard that I found poignant in the face of these fears of mine:

"Father in heaven! You hold all the good gifts in your gentle hand. Give everyone his allotted share as it is well pleasing to you. And give everyone the assurance that everything comes from you, so that joy will not tear us away from you in the forgetfulness of pleasure, so that sorrow will not separate you from us, but in joy we may go to you and in sorrow remain with you. And when our days are numbered and our outer being is wasted away, grant that death may not come in its own name, cold and terrible, but gentle and friendly with greetings and news, with witness from you, our heavenly Father! [7]

In the end what is our life but a love story filled with triumph and tragedy, of hearts aspiring, rising, suffering and being crushed and rising again. With all of our longings and desires, we seek to bridge the chasms that define our "not good" aloneness, reaching out to each other and by grace, reaching up to God. How wonderful that in our longing we discover that God is first reaching in our direction, summoning us to love, to be great lovers of God and our fellow humans, to love with all the passion of love's risks and rewards hanging in the balance.

Chapter XLVIII

So Far, and So Far Yet To Go

I became a Christian through the death of someone else's son. I have become a deeper and more peaceful one through the death of my own. In some mystical, unexplainable way, my sorrows have united me to the heart of Father, Son, and Holy Spirit. It is a union that is deeply personal and significant. I have been awarded the dignity of sharing the sufferings within the heart of God. My losses have been enormous. My consolations have been tender and magnificent. My gains are pure gold!

This little volume has been a labor of love and a tale of love lost and love reborn. I have lost the privilege of loving my youngest son up close; I must now love him through the mists of time, waiting to see him face to face until I too make the crossing to the land beyond time. But love him still I do, perhaps more passionately now than when he was with me here on earth. It is also an incomplete chronicle of the love of a husband for his beloved wife as it has passed through a blast furnace of sorrow and emerged not only with stronger steel as its frame, but with much refined gold in its heart. There is here also just an inkling of the concern in a very human father's heart for the lives of his children who remain, and for their children who are coming along and growing so rapidly. Their sorrow is never far from the sphere of my concern for them. I long for each one of them to know my love for them and my pride in them. I pray for them to each live a full and faith-filled life, and that their own trials and sorrows will teach them as much as mine have taught me.

And I have written for all those who have lost someone dear to them in the hopes that the sharing of my struggles will in some small way bring a measure of healing. I pray that the awful experience of feeling abandoned and of being totally alone will be diminished, even if ever so slightly, so that those who suffer might at least hear the footsteps of another who is walking on the dusty road with them, and might hear the voice of a fellow griever who cries in the wilderness, "Prepare the way for the Lord." I wish you healing and hope, my fellow sufferers.

And lastly, this has been the story of my wrestling match with the great lover of my soul, who sought me and bought me with the price of his own life laid down. Jesus, who suffered and died for me, has never deserved my anger nor my accusations, but in my lostness, I hurled them in his direction because I knew of no place else to throw them. He has patiently loved me toward healing in spite of my misplaced anger and my despairing disappointment which I blamed on him. Everything I have laid upon him he has born, without returning recrimination. Surely he has born my grief and carried my sorrows. By his stripes I am being healed. He has not been counting my transgressions against his sacred heart. He has never ceased to welcome my wounds into his presence, no matter what form they took when they arrived. Jesus has been my Lord and my faithful friend. He has given me assurances that my dear son is safe home. He is perfecting in me the peace that passes all of my capacity to understand it. What has gone on between us, and what continues to unfold is a passionate love story in which the great lover is Jesus himself. I am the object of a love and affection which I don't deserve and one which I can never earn. I am living in sheer Grace, in the unmerited favor of my Lord and my God. Thanks be to His holy and precious name.

Chapter XLVII

A Small Prayer Book

Prayer of thanks for the trust of fellow grievers:

Father, I am deeply humbled and privileged when your people in sorrow invite me onto the holy ground of their grief. It is such a risky business to let imperfect people like me come near. I feel unworthy of such trust, which indeed I am. But I know that what each one is really seeking is comfort from you. So I enter in, confident that you go before me and will shepherd the encounter in a healing direction. Your compassion is powerful and you never fail to meet people in the way that they can receive you, if only their hearts have been prepared by your Spirit working deeply within them, through their tears. Grant me to be sensitive, caring, and listening. Allow me to be a tangible expression of your presence with whomever I meet in the pit of sorrow. And when I fail, may they know that it was never my intent to add to their burden, and may they be able to forgive me. I ask this in your name, Lord Jesus. Amen.

Prayers for special days:

Dear Lord, Today marks the anniversary of my child's (or other loved one's) death. A flood of memories and emotions all rise up to meet me as I arise. Lord, I remember the gift of *his* life with such a mixture of longing and gratitude. I long to see *him*, and to greet *him* with a passionate embrace that will erase the distance now between us. These longings I must endure without relief. Show me today Lord some sign of your Grace that I may do more than endure mutely the sorrow that has been my soul's constant companion. Help me to recall with thanksgiving all the fond memories I have of *him.* Such recollection not only intensifies my sadness, which it does, but also increases gratitude within me, which is the most sure path toward healing that I know. Be present with me in each hour and minute of this day. I pray in your name, Lord Jesus Christ. Amen.

Merry Christmas! Lord, how shall we be merry in this land of exile, in the foreign land of sorrow? Here in the midst of holiday festivities we hang up our instruments of praise, while our captor, The Great Sadness, implores us to sing one of the songs of the season: Deck the Halls; tis the season to be jolly, fa la la la la. Joy to the world! How can we sing now that our hearts have been rent in pain and loss? We remember the prophecy given by Simeon to your own mother: "And a sword will pierce your own soul." And pierce her it did. Now we have joined her company, the company of those who have lost a beloved child in death. We ache to return to life as it was before this awful fork in the road that has separated us from "normal" existence. From the path we are on there is no turning back. Help us Lord to move forward, inching ever closer to you, Immanuel, God with us. Be with us today and teach us to celebrate through our tears. We thank you for coming and being born. You are the only light in our dark world. Bring your promised peace on earth, and give us in our grief-ravaged hearts, the peace that passes all understanding, through Jesus Christ we pray. Amen.

A birthday prayer:

Lord, today was the day that your miracle came into the world. *She* **was such a delight to our eyes. From the moment we laid eyes on** *her she* **was the delight of our hearts. We raised** *her* **with love and with care. We watched and cheered as** *she* **learned to crawl, then walk, to read and draw and write.** *She* **grew before us, and we grew with** *her. She* **made us vulnerable in frighteningly deep regions of our souls. We celebrated** *her* **birthdays through all the years we had** *her* **here with us. Now we observe the day with the painful mixture of sadness and emptiness. We hope to see** *her* **again in eternity where life is celebrated every moment in your presence. Amen.**

Prayer for alertness:

Father, you well know how in times past I have passed by on the other side of the road when someone was lying in the ditch of loss. I have been far too occupied with my own priorities and crammed agenda. In my busyness, I have failed to hear the cries of many afflicted people. Forgive me. I pray for a new awareness of those grieving ones whom you place in my path. I know that I can not respond to all who are in sorrow in the world, but I do not want to miss the ones that you bring to me by your divine appointment. Give me ears to hear and eyes to see, so that I may not miss the blessing of being your hands, feet, and heart in this world that is filled with so much anguish. I pray in the name that is above every name, the precious name of Jesus. Amen.

Prayer for Continuing On:

Dear Lord, I know not where this journey will go from here on. But one thing I know for sure; I will not walk it alone. You have promised to be with me always and I believe your word. In the times of my sorrows, I will call to you for comfort. In the night when I am afraid, I will

summon the strength of your Spirit to calm my heart and return me to my center of strength in you When I become disoriented and confused I will seek your wisdom which you give generously and graciously to those who ask. And when death visits again, I will have confidence in the power of life over death, and I will bear witness to all who will listen that in you is life forevermore. Thanks be to you, dear Lord Jesus. There is none like you in heaven or on earth. Amen.

Perhaps you have never given your heart to Christ and would like to do so. Here is a sample prayer for getting started:

Jesus, I have never called you Lord. I have been going my own way, living my life as seemed best to me. I have tried to be a decent human being, but I have come to realize that I need something deeper than my own efforts to be a good person. This sorrow has put me in the grip of something so big that I have grown weary of trying to survive from day to day. I need you and the help that only you can give. I am sorry that it took me so long to call out for you, to come to you, to realize that I need you and that for all this time your love for me seemed unreal and unnecessary. Forgive my sins and presumption. Set me free from the futility of life apart from you. In your mercy, come into my heart and take up residence there. So far as I am able, I surrender all my thoughts, my emotions, my imagination, my affections, and my will to you now. Take me as I am and change me as only you can. Thank you for making me aware of your promises of forgiveness and kindness to one such as me, and thank you for finally bringing me to the place where I am willing to receive life from you. Jesus, I humbly ask that you hear my prayer and grant my petitions in your name. Amen.

Perhaps you gave your heart to the Lord in the past, but the sorrow has damaged your relationship with Him and you desire restoration. Here is a suggested prayer to get you started:

Lord, I have been furious with you, with the world, and with life and with death. I have shut myself off from trust, from faith, and from hope. I have inhabited the grey land, the land of despair, and the land of self defense. I have been crouching like a wounded dog, snarling at anyone who comes near, including you. I realize that I am being devoured by my own bitterness and that I need deliverance. Come Lord Jesus, forgive, have mercy upon me, and set me free to love you again. My needs are so great they are beyond my ability to see them clearly enough to describe them to you. I must now, and do now, present myself to you for the healing of our relationship. Underneath it all, I know that you alone are my most precious friend and without you I am lost forever. Hear my cry and be swift to my aid. This I pray in your name. Amen.

Or if despair has not been your predominant emotion, you might pray something like this:

Jesus, my faith which once seemed so vibrant and alive, so full of confidence and promise, now seems grey and lifeless. I feel so disappointed to the point of being faithless. I need a faith from you, a deeper faith that does not depend upon my ability to sustain it, a faith that comes as a gift and remains as a gift. What I'm saying Lord is that I need your help and your deliverance. Please do not consign me to the shadow lands of my own failed efforts to believe. I believe, help me through my unbelief, and bring me to the place where all my hope is once again in you, in your name I pray, Amen.

And finally, healing, restoration, and the ability to trust all come down to choices. We must choose to once more praise the

Lord, to give thanks, to acknowledge that despite all we've been through, His steadfast love endures forever. The Psalms are full of such prayers. Allow me to add one of my own:

Lord, today I will praise you from the pit of sorrow. Let my praises surmount the canyon walls of grief that have hemmed me in and kept me soaking upon a bed of tears. I confess that praise is the last thing I feel like doing, but I am choosing to praise you in spite of how I feel. I confess that the months and years since my son's death have been filled with lamentation, with tormenting questions and haunting doubts. My praises have been faint and have seemed hollow. But your relentless love has stayed by my side; no, rather you have remained alive in the deepest recesses of my heart, your presence living deeper than even my tears and sorrow. You are the bedrock of my life.

Once again, you have mastered despair and death with the sheer force of your life and your love. I praise you. I lift your name up, higher and higher with each passing day. Accept the praises I bring. They are offered from the depth of a wounded heart that has once again learned to be thankful for all your goodness to me. May each one of my companions in trials receive the same extravagant comfort that I have received from you. With love and renewed faith in you Lord Jesus Christ, Bill

Chapter XLVIII

Another Avalon Son Rise

Journal entry: April 10th, 2010

Dear Jon,
Today would have been your 29th birthday. I now call my insomniac nights "old man's disease" since I know so many men who have trouble sleeping through the night after they pass 60. As I lay awake at 3 this morning, I was thinking of you. Just yesterday, mom and I were wondering if today would be particularly sad. We've both learned that we just never know what to expect on any day. We are now, after nearly five years, battle-hardened grievers. We know the drill all too well at this point.
Anyway, I was thinking in the darkness that your birthdays now are sort of irrelevant. In the nearly five years since you have been "safe home" you must have become a vastly different man than when you left. I'm guessing you'll have to introduce yourself to me when I get there and we will have eternity to really get to know each other in all of our perfected glory.
Once again, I am in Avalon, writing at sunrise. You are never far from our thoughts and we carry you along in our hearts. Love never ends as Paul wrote to the Corinthians with such inspired insight. You may remember that Neal Young wrote a

song, *"Only love can break your heart."* Yes; and only love can heal it too. Your great lover and ours, our Lord Jesus, has been diligently loving us back to joy and pulling us forward through our sorrow over you and establishing us in the hope of one day seeing you again.

It's taken me these five years to be substantially healed. I now am mostly filled with gratitude and with joy in living again. I've learned to carry your memory along with me and to let the sadness minister to me. Grief has been a powerful teacher of things I would never have learned in any other way.

Your memory *"keeps me awake and alive"* as our mutually favorite song of Peter Gabriel's so aptly put it. Austin so insightfully described you as the silent prophet of hope. Your silence and the force of your life which fuels my longing to see you once more indeed spurs me on to hope deeply in all the promises of God. My faith is renewed. Though older physically, inside I am young again. When you left, maybe you sprinkled my soul with the magic of your youthful passion on your way out the door. I just couldn't see it while I was buried under the avalanche of grief. I have emerged back into the light of day. Another sunrise has occurred over the Atlantic Ocean and I am grateful to be here to witness another day on my way to being where you are.

Dear Jon, I will love you until we meet on another shore and we both stand together in the light of God's Son, our Savior and Lord.

With undying love,
Dad

ChapterXLXIX

Afterword, by Dr. Austin Joyce, Counselor and Friend to Both Jon and to Me

Jon,

I have just finished reading your dad's manuscript. It is a tender, gut wrenching, and hope filled remembrance of a journey for him and your mother through the "valley of the shadow of death". (Psalm 23:6) Little did I know how blessed I was to spend the time together with you as you invited me into the hell of your addiction and your irrepressible longing for a sanctuary of love. As you well know, addicts discover that the raw power of fear, terror, anxiety, shame, and a craving for love can never be relieved through artificial means, chemical or otherwise. Well did you live the words of the Apostle Paul: "The things I don't want to do, I do; I don't seem able to do the things that I want."

Your Body bore witness to the savage attack of chemical opiates, psychological terrors, and relentless fears. Yet through it all, you never gave up hope. Dogged in your determination to fight this all consuming killer, you struggled each day with sobriety. You came to my office, session after session, driving an hour each way. You were always "present" and passionately searching with me for anchors to ground your wandering spirit. "One day at a time" was not a cliché for you. Moment to moment, breath to breath, you never knew if you would be sober for a minute, an hour, or a day. You courageously attacked denial's illusory invitation to a chemical wonderland. You fought the monster which "prowled about like a roaring lion seeking someone to devour." (I Peter)

You lived explosively each day. There was no holding back. If there was a safety net it was not for you. You lived fully aware of life's fragility and you loved nonetheless. You weren't afraid of living, even when you weren't quite sure how to do it. In one of your dad's prayers above he wrote, "I humble myself before Your perfect will and plan. Deliver me from false paths to false comforts that lead to dead ends filled with dead things." He saw into your soul in a way that at times was frightening and confirming for you. Unfortunately, your humble, fragile spirit got sucked into one last dead end which you never intended.

When your dad asked me to deliver the homily at your funeral service I didn't want to do it. I love your parents as I loved you. I was upset and angry, not at you but at the sting of death that none of us could control. I hated the loss of your temporal life. Nonetheless, I was drawn into the sheer grace exposed in your heart and borrowed from your passion the will to see what the Spirit was unfolding in you, the "silent prophet." You lived in the tension between death's destructive force and the power of eternal life. Your life was not wasted, just cruelly shortened. I don't claim to understand God's providential presence in all of this. Your death created a void through which we all are walking from grace to grace.

In 30 years of pastoral and clinical work, I have had glimpses of grace. Through your passion I felt the pulse of the divine out of the depths of your pain. You knew that your addiction was wild and out of control, as was the grief of your parents after your passing. Your death shattered the illusion of control and certainty about the issues of life. It raised many questions for your parents and friends, such as, "What is the point of your life, and of ours?" The question is too big for me. I only know that you were a prophet of hope however silenced your voice is now.

As your dad wrote and most of us realized, at least briefly, "We live life blindly and take far too much for granted." The Bible reminds the careful pursuer of God that God's enemy and ours seeks not love but death. The evil one tried time and time again to snatch you out of the heart of God. Nevertheless your death was not the devil's victory but your gateway back into the heart of God.

When we were together I was impressed by your searching mind, passionate heart, and fragile spirit, all draped by a sheer grace which could be so easily pushed aside by the tentacles of addiction. In spite of this, you always risked hope. In the midst of your daily struggles and your parents' fears and frustrations, hope bound you together. Your dad rediscovered through his grief that "it is hard to be blessed and play it safe all at once." Jon, you knew better than any of us that your life on this earth could not be safe, however much your parents desired it. You didn't believe in safety because you sensed in your spirit that your journey was not, nor would it ever be, safe. Safety is not for a prophet of God.

Hope was the guarantee you carried. You never truly believed that chemicals were the solution to the quest for hope in your soul. Your dad wrote about this reality when he said, "the illusion of control and self-determination" plagues our nation and our world. Your life and death exposed all who knew you to the reality that our journey can offer, through sheer grace, the truth of God who is with us, even when we walk through the valley of the shadow of death.

Your dad's courage to ask what your life meant led him to realize that "you touched a lot of people in your short life." Your dad's gutsy, ruthless self examination has gently woven the delicate fabric of love and grief and reveals for whoever may walk through the valley of suffering the roller coaster ride of hope and faith, trust and rage, truth and helplessness, and ultimately sheds light on the love of God to pilgrims along this arduous path. As your parents walk through "the slow relentless process of being stripped," they are discovering out of their dark night an evolving peace and presence that for now can only be lightly touched. Your dad's reflection is a testimony of hope as was your life.

As he wrote above, "I still miss you my son, so very much, and am still moved to tears. In fact, I am more alive now even in my sadness. It is good to feel the full range of emotions, even when they are wild and unimaginable. Thank you Lord for being with me, my constant friend and lover of my soul. Amen."

So my beloved friend, the silent prophet of hope, continue your intercessions for your family and friends as we continue through the valley of tears toward the glory you now know. I pray this book goes forth into the hands and hearts of many, "reaching out to each other and by sheer grace, reaching up to God as God reaches down to us."

With thanksgiving, Shalom,
Austin

Acknowledgements

Many of the people to whom I owe a deep debt of gratitude are mentioned in the text above; many are not. I fear that were I to try to list them all, I would certainly miss some and if I didn't, this would end up reading like a page in the phone book. So, thanks to one and all.

I do want to extend a special thanks to Gerry and Jennifer O'Malley for their kind and generous hospitality in letting me come repeatedly to their vacation home on the Jersey shore in Avalon. Their home away from home has been the place where I have returned repeatedly to seek the Lord, to rest and be refreshed, to pray, and to write. Most of this manuscript was composed there, within earshot of the waves of the Atlantic Ocean. May God richly bless you both and thank you from the bottom of my heart.

And thanks to my beloved wife Jean for all your courage and patience and support. You're the best!

End Notes

1. <u>Provocations: The Spiritual Writings of Kierkegaard.</u> Plough Publishing, 1999; Charles Moore, ed. P. 384

2. ibid.

3 <u>An Old Woman's Reflections, Peig</u> Sayers, Oxford University Press. 2000 Reissue, p.101

4. <u>A Pity Youth Does Not Last,</u> Michael O'Guiheen. Oxford University Press, 2000 Reissue. p.112-113.

5. Peter Gabriel, Geffen Records, 1986

6. <u>Provocations,</u> p. 260

7. ibid. p.349

CPSIA information can be obtained
at www.ICGtesting.com
Printed in the USA
LVHW111416280220
648524LV00001B/112